by Marilyn Vickrage

Now I Remember Who I Am

BALBOA PRESS
A DIVISION OF HAY HOUSE

Copyright © 2012 Marilyn Vickrage

All rights reserved. No part of this book may be used or reproduced by any means, graphic, electronic, or mechanical, including photocopying, recording, taping or by any information storage retrieval system without the written permission of the publisher except in the case of brief quotations embodied in critical articles and reviews.

Balboa Press books may be ordered through booksellers or by contacting:

Balboa Press
A Division of Hay House
1663 Liberty Drive
Bloomington, IN 47403
www.balboapress.com.au
1-(877) 407-4847

ISBN: 978-1-4525-0586-2 (sc)
ISBN: 978-1-4525-0587-9 (e)

Because of the dynamic nature of the Internet, any web addresses or links contained in this book may have changed since publication and may no longer be valid. The views expressed in this work are solely those of the author and do not necessarily reflect the views of the publisher, and the publisher hereby disclaims any responsibility for them.

The author of this book does not dispense medical advice or prescribe the use of any technique as a form of treatment for physical, emotional, or medical problems without the advice of a physician, either directly or indirectly. The intent of the author is only to offer information of a general nature to help you in your quest for emotional and spiritual well-being. In the event you use any of the information in this book for yourself, which is your constitutional right, the author and the publisher assume no responsibility for your actions.

Printed in the United States of America

Balboa Press rev. date: 09/07/2012

CONTENTS

Preface vii
Chapter 1: Opening the door to your heart 1
Chapter 2: Simply Channeling 7
Chapter 3: One with all 11
Chapter 4: All part of the plan 16
Chapter 5: In the stillness of the moment 25
Chapter 6: Surrendering 33
Chapter 7: Live courageously 39
Chapter 8: Accepting responsibility 45
Chapter 9: You need to wake up 52
Chapter 10: Being is enough 57
Chapter 11: The illusion of separateness 62
Chapter 12: Taking care of your vehicle 69
Chapter 13: Balancing your life 76
Chapter 14: I came with a purpose 82
Chapter 15: Greatness is your birthright 90
Chapter 16: Knowing your empowered self 96
Chapter 17: Being unstoppable 102
Chapter 18: Begin by practicing 108
Chapter 19: Children are our teachers 114
Chapter 20: We are all intuitive facilitators 119
Chapter 21: Abundance in all its forms 126
Chapter 22: Whales are calling 133
Chapter 23: Peace on earth 138
Chapter 24: Love is what truly matters 145
Chapter 25: Perception 152
Endnotes 159

PREFACE

Spread the word, that life is sweet, eternal, loving and abundant, and nothing else

I BECAME OPEN TO RECEIVING messages of love, hope and inspiration several years ago, at a time in my life when I was really struggling with events and circumstances playing out around me. Feelings of desperation often besieged me and I hungered to maintain balance everyday, some how. I was determined to find peace within me so that I could step through the difficulties I found myself facing on a daily basis. I could not solve the issues alone and it was then that I deferred to a higher being, my divine higher self.

I felt as if I was trapped in a situation that was out of my control, no solutions in sight, and at times I could barely breath from the persistent anxiety arising within me. I felt desperate and very far removed from my comfort level. The nervousness I felt was overwhelming and I was more than ready to stop and listen to my still inner voice for it was time for me to really pay attention to what it said. It was a profound moment, because up until then I had chosen to ignore the soft voice within me that spoke very loudly, of being far greater than I could possibly conceive of, let alone accept. I chose to risk it all, for I had nothing to lose, my world was in chaos, or so I thought.

Initially, it took great courage for me to sit quietly and listen to that gentle, reassuring voice, for I had to break through layer upon layer of fearful emotions, which generally spoke to me much louder than my unconditional loving self. I knew there was a part of me that yearned to express it self, the larger than life aspect of me who knows everything. Yet, for years I deliberately evaded that journey of expansion into the inner realms of being. Each time I thought about expressing that knowledge, my apprehension of being rejected, scoffed at, ridiculed and embarrassed, immediately surfaced to sabotage my intention.

On some level it was inevitable and the timing was right for me to open the door to my heart and seriously take notice to what it said. From that centeredness, I connected with love, unconditional love, and the messages that I received were truly inspiring. I met myself face to face, and fully realized that "I" was far more than anything perceived and imagined with logical thinking. I touched core feelings of bliss that brought tears of elation and happiness flooding through my entire being. All problems were swept away as nonexistent in that quiet, yet powerfully energetic place of stillness where the all-pervasive life essence emanates from.

At the heart of it all, I had chosen to trust myself implicitly and so the journey began. I let go, more and more, and allowed the expressions and feelings to surge through me onto the pages and was overawed by the simple truthfulness that resonated from within and throughout my being. The words reassured me that everything was perfect, now and always, as it is in reality. I reunited with who I am, a powerful being, an essential part of the totality of creation. The messages inspired me to stay centered and live each moment lovingly, even whilst the swirling storm of events ran rampant and out of control around me. Not knowing how to fix my outer world, I discovered that I was able to live peacefully from within, connecting with the source of infinite being.

The transcripts written throughout the book are exactly as I received them, word for word, and my purpose in passing this loving information on is to inspire and enable you to unite within to abundant love, peace and harmony, manifesting it outwardly into your world, no matter how it appears externally. No matter how many problems or traumas seem to exist for you in your daily life. They are the illusion that we have learnt to focus on, rather than seeing the beauty of life from the inside out. I rejoice in offering these touching messages to you, linking with your hearts to assist you on your path of discovery and realization of who you are.

It has been an absolute marvel for me to compose this beautiful book, one that mirrors my inner being, my darkness and my light. I never imagined the wealth of knowledge and wisdom I had at my fingertips, or that the words and more specifically the life force beyond the words, would grant me such deep insights into myself. It has truly been an immense privilege for me to undertake this awakening evolution of myself, and I continually and constantly grow in faith, and in compassion and understanding.

I am especially grateful for having such an empathetic and loving ally in Lee my husband, for there were times when the content channelled appeared to be of such a sacred nature that I questioned my ability to pass it along for others to read. My self-doubt was highlighted in those moments, and it was then that I realized my ego was getting in the way of my progression. At times I was my own worst enemy and thankfully the support and encouragement I received from Lee motivated me to move beyond *thinking* and to continue *being one in the moment* with the task.

Eternal thanks also to my wonderful children for their constant love and resonance, my daughter Heidi, always steadfast in reminding me to keep going during the times I was distracted and my life seemed to take another direction. And to my son Nick for his cool appraisal once I had finished, of letting it go and trusting that the work will take care of itself.

Much love and thanks to dear friends Fleur, and Elliott (now in spirit) who would always enquire about the progress of the book and were very eager to read the finished product. To my wonderful friend Sue for all our deep and meaningful conversations, whose heart is on the same page as mine, and to Marde for his generosity and creative insights into the creation of the book cover.

Over the years, I have had many wonderful mentors, in many places far and wide, and in many forms, both human and in spirit. I am very thankful for the lessons and the opportunities each one has presented me. Every occasion has provided a step up the ladder of self-awareness and of embracing my true worth, and as those who offered their services to me, I now offer mine.

It is my very purpose, to be a bright and shining star
to lighten up a darkened night,
inspiring love to glow a hue of brilliant, blinding majesty,
that which appears to be outside, amazingly resides within,
such wondrous beauty can only be sought
in the silent recesses of the heart,
in perfect harmony with life's majestic serenade.

CHAPTER ONE

Opening the door to your heart

*Open the door to your heart and let the loving light shine
forth into your life in radiant abundance*

My wakeup call arrived early one bright and beautiful autumn morning, when I least expected it. In fact it was a monumental turning point in my life, particularly the way in which I viewed it. I had just driven my partner Lee to work and I was feeling very relaxed as I made my way back along the beautiful scenic drive winding down towards my home at the beach. As I drove in quiet reverie, I felt inspired to visit one of my closest and oldest friends, Fleur. Her home is on a magnificent tropical fruit farm, with sweeping views to the coast and surrounding hinterland and I had to pass by it on my homeward journey. We had been friends for many, many years and over time our relationship had blossomed into a very special, spiritual congeniality. We both had a common interest in the metaphysical and our friendship had spanned a lifetime of sharing personal experiences, exchanging books and chatting about the wonders and beauty of life. We connected on a deep and mutual level of understanding and had a very easy-going, fun relationship with each other.

On entering the fully glass enclosed living area of Fleur's country home, I could feel the heat from the sun streaming through the panes, warming the air and creating a welcoming ambience. The room overlooked a magnificent rural panorama, and I could sense the peace and serenity exuding its presence as I seated myself on one of the comfy leather chairs clustered around the room. Relaxing fully, I scanned the beautiful collection of angel pieces which adorned every table and shelf in the room, and which Fleur loved immensely. It was quite obvious to me that she was an angel herself, of the earthly type, and my glance also fell to the ever-increasing packs of angel cards that were spread throughout the room in many small groupings. Fleur had motivated me years earlier to delve into angel readings by gifting me a pack for my birthday. Every morning without fail, I would sit up in bed, shuffle the cards and be exhilarated by the message. I found it to be a wonderful way to begin the new day, and still do.

As we sat happily chatting, it became apparent that Fleur was leading into the same question she often asked me, "Have you started writing your book yet Marilyn, I had a vision of you writing only yesterday?" As was my usual response I replied, "When the time is right", however as soon as the words had been uttered, I had a deep sense that today was different. Now was different. Little did I realize that I was about to open the door to a whole new world of stimulation and self-expression, far beyond anything I could have ever imagined. Fleur reached down and picked up one of her latest decks of the beautifully illustrated cards and pushed them into my hands. Whilst I was shuffling, I considered what she had said regarding her vision of me writing and I realized that I had held that dream in my heart for many, many years, as if it was a part of my very essence. Now, I could clearly see the book already finished, an inspirational best seller, with words of wisdom scattered throughout the pages, and those thoughts sent feelings of elation sweeping through me.

Abruptly a card flew out of my hands and fell into my lap. As I picked it up the words opened to my vision, snapping my attention back into the moment. It was a brilliantly depicted card, of a glorious angel, and defined by its own unique message. As I have always found when ever I use the cards, the statement resonates with my energy and emotions in that moment and being no exception, the words so appropriately prompted me to think about beginning what I had never started. My entire body responded with gentle, tingling goose bumps that ran up and down my spine. Instantly I knew, without a shadow of a doubt, that it was time for me to embark upon writing my book. The certainty hit me like a giant wave rolling over my body and I felt as if I was being guided to make a shift within myself to begin the task, even though I had absolutely no idea what I was going to put in writing. As I left Fleur's house shortly after, feelings of excitement began to well up within me, along with a great sense of commitment and urgency energizing my being. I knew that no matter what words came flowing through me, it was the right time to begin and how it would unfold would be the journey I had dreamt of making for over twenty five years.

Arriving home extremely buoyed up, I eagerly searched for and found an old, scrappy pad, and with pen in hand I sat down ready to begin. I closed my eyes and breathed deeply, allowing my thoughts to slowly subside until I felt very calm, clearing all mental chatter that could disturb me in my purpose. I felt that in this relaxed state, the words would surely pour out easily onto the pages. And they did. Since learning meditation at an early age, I had developed the ability to go deeply into a state of stillness whenever the need had arisen, dispelling stress in my mind and body, particularly after experiencing arguments with my partner or children. When overwhelmed by negative emotions swirling through me and feeling a need for my own breathing space, I would simply head for the bathroom or toilet. Shutting the door behind me so that no one would interrupt me, I would sit on the toilet lid slowly breathing in and exhaling out until I could feel my body and mind releasing the built up tension, completely soothed in the process. In this quiet sanctum, I found the space and place within me to let it all go and centre myself in peace once again.

Now as I comfortably sat ready to permit the message to come, I asked my loving self for the graciousness to guide me in the process. Immediately the expressions sprang clearly into my mind and I began to write, astonished by the prompt response to my question. It was as though the floodgates had burst open and years of holding back fell away, allowing the transcription to run almost faster than I could keep pace with. When they came no longer, I looked down at the pad to see that I had actually scribbled more than six pages. My hand felt totally numb, but I felt jubilant, beyond comprehension. I had at last committed myself to the task and had been honoured by the natural flowing language that had spoken to me so beautifully, as if it had a mind of its own. Such a perfect spiritual connection, I understood that I had opened my heart and mind to receive the flood of information that followed.

Feelings overwhelmed me and I began to cry tears of absolute happiness, and relief, as my heart opened in ecstasy and I felt an infinite supply of love and support pouring into my being. I understood that I had been firmly self protective for fear of failing, of not being good enough and that those old, familiar emotions had stopped me from beginning writing years earlier. I had always thought and convinced myself, until then, that I was not capable or worthy of such an achievement. I sat quietly for a long time, absorbing the heightened feeling of loving presence radiating through my entirety. I felt as if I was glowing and had just awoken to the life force within me, allowing the divine spirit to surge freely, expanding my awareness and knowledge. It felt divine. Trusting myself, I had at last manifested in form, that which had been locked within me. Finally I looked down at the pages to reveal the words that had appeared so powerfully through me, and I was amazed at what I read. It was as though they had always been a part of me, imprinted in my being, a blueprint of who I was and the message was profound.

I was left speechless, and at the same time awestruck by the ancient text and writings, for it was as though the terminology came from a place of deep understanding and knowledge within me, from some other time long past where truth was known to all. My heart swelled with loving feelings of gratitude, for I had at last dropped the mantle of fear that had held me back and allowed my self to open the door to my heart in communion with the divine living force inherent within. I was astonished by the familiarity and the unconditional love I felt; it was a meeting with my higher self.

Message:

> The word is God and God is the word. Let all men know that there is no other, nor anything else that exists. This is the truth. There is only that which exists in this time and place now, where each one sits and breaths the air. All else is misguided and an illusion. Once this is sought more than now, it will change the vibration of the earth and entities that live on it.

> There exists no other plan but this one simple law. So return to the plan and be pleased with life as it is and not as you think it should be. There is a simple process for doing this, and it is called manna1. It has long stood the test of time and it is the only path. It is very simply arrived at by looking within instead of without. You all know this simple law, yet you have forgotten

the simplicity. Be guided by your loving hearts and not only by your silly heads.

Only love exists and it is in this essence that all life exists in magnificent radiance. If you only knew how magnificent it all is, then fear would be swept away in an instant, to be replaced with overwhelming feelings of love and gratitude. And blessing each other as brothers and sisters of the light, then peace and harmony would always prevail. To hurt another in any way would be to hurt ones self.

What joy and blessings would follow and then life on earth would be so bountiful that heaven would prevail and all life would live gratefully, well pleased that each and everyone was always sustained in love.

You are a miracle; we are all miracles of the splendour of love. We are not here to struggle and fight, but for the purpose of joyful reunion with each other. That is the plan, to reunite you all with the one source of love, which is life eternal. Oh, what a blessing, with this we can achieve anything, and in the knowing only comes more love and prosperity for each entity as it reunites with itself.

Abundant love is the key and there is no other way. It all comes down to joining up the dots like a puzzle, and continuing to join until the few become one in harmony with the divine plan of unity. Unity brings happiness, cooperation and continuance of a wonderful society of such loving beings that the earth has ever seen and felt since its existence.

A miracle is the fact that once you all discover your true identities and allow for the union that must take place, as it is inevitable and what you all planned even before your arrival; you will indeed all live the lives that you are now searching to live. It is this simple. Come back to your home, which is in your heart, and discover your true essence and energy. There you shall find peace both of mind and heart.

As you think, so you are; turn off the head and turn on the heart. Let God's loving presence, which is your very essence, flow abundantly through your veins and renew every cell with health and vitality, youth and vigor. The giant within will emerge, free and ready for action.

Be aware of your head space (thoughts) that love to throw you a challenge at every opportunity. The self chatter is "feeling left out" and merely wants to bring you back to its attention, and it is very good at this, in fact it excels at keeping most of you completely in the dark and way off track from discovering your true selves. Do not be disillusioned by the seemingly silly things that come into your head. You are able to tell the difference between what is true and what is not. You feel it in your heart and it beats loudly in your very essence and you open to the resonance of its truth.

Open your hearts dear ones and allow your lights to shine. Unlock the door and take a peak inside and discover your magnificent self. Allow yourself to be swept into the infinite loving energy of creation, and to lead you to the next level of your soul's purpose on earth; to create peace, for one and all.

Building one another up, not tearing each other down is the catch cry of the spirit and this is the truth of loving your fellow man, as yourself. When you feel this in your heart, you make the deliberate decision to stop playing out the old, entrenched patterns that do not serve you or anyone else in your life. You begin the journey of stepping off the old path and moving onto an exciting new path of self love, respect and honour.

To respect and honour your self means an end to attracting people towards you who do not vibrate to your own energy level. As on the inside, so it is on the outside.

Inner Guidance:

Make a declaration, to choose only goodness into your life, and begin by showering all others with goodness from your heart. Great beauty comes from great heart.

CHAPTER TWO

Simply Channeling

Do nothing, stop and know your self

THE NEXT DAY FOLLOWING MY open connection with spirit, I could hardly wait to repeat it and to express more of the grand communiqué again. I felt exhilarated, as never before and at the same time a little anxious, for what if my heart had shut the door and the words did not come? Would they pour forth as easily as they had the day before? There was only one way to find out. As I settled myself comfortably on the couch, clearing my mind of unnecessary thought, the exact scenario transpired, without hesitation and soon the pages were full of wondrous information being delivered at the same rapid pace. Again, I was astonished at the clarity and power of the message, profusely simple. My *active* relationship with spirit was alive like never before and it guided me to pen without consciously knowing what followed. I felt a loving, safe presence permeating my entire being and I wanted to understand if it was my soul or another energetic being directing the process.

Over the years I had spent many, many occasions contemplating how I would begin, what would it feel like to let down my guard and surrender to a meld of spirit and human endeavor, of channeling. I had previously recognized my ruminations as a 'Search for the Truth', reflecting my intense curiosity for the meaning of life. Most times it had seemed such a huge assignment and something beyond my individual capacity. My mind would be constantly trying to come up with excuses for not taking the task seriously, and so the sabotage would be complete and finally I would give up in exasperation and scrap the idea. This was a regular pattern I began to witness myself acting out and eventually, as always, I would cave into the crushing mind control. I figured that if it was to happen, the procedure would unfold more readily, making the work an enjoyable one, not the struggle I was grappling with each time I tried to make it happen. In hindsight, it was my deep fear of connecting with the unknown, unseen energy of spirit and a very real sense of trepidation of conjuring up dark demons into my life. Particularly of allowing my ego to take control by continually giving me reasons to remain in fear.

Now however, the alignment felt complete, and I knew in my heart that I was being guided to channel. It felt absolutely divinely propelled, and perfectly safe. One of my greatest dreams had always been to motivate myself and other people to greatness and here I was now feeling totally enlivened by the energy flowing through me, *inspiring me greatly*. I realized that in trusting, and simply being still was all that was necessary. My thoughts, which generally would have been offering up a bounty of excuses, were set aside and my full attention was totally in the present moment, with the simple task at hand of allowing myself to receive the data. Having faith in the process was providing me with the energy and capacity to convey the words to paper, in a very natural and spontaneous way. I was an open vessel, ready and willing to accept that which was being delivered through me. I knew the association I was having with myself was deeply spiritual, infinitely intelligent and it felt amazing. I understood perfectly the saying, 'get out of your own way' and by doing so, I was permitting the fuel of supply to run freely without hindrance from an over zealous ego. I realized it was all-powerful and purposeful in every way and I had no need to understand it logically. It was purely happening in natural flow with my non-resistance. Whether it was I, another spiritual entity or being was of no relevance to the outpouring of the message, it was simply about letting go and receiving, and being absolutely accepting of the procedure.

I had previously had the greatest pleasure of being in company with Lee Caroll who is the original channel for Kryon[2] and a very loving human being. During my time at Mt Shasta, it was a delight to explore first hand the process of a Spiritual entity blending with a Human entity. It truly was a melding of heart and spirit and the stream of loving presence was obvious. My attraction to travel across oceans for first-hand understanding of the practice was beyond my logical comprehension. It did though, seem part of the plan to gain insights into a far-reaching wisdom, not only held within my consciousness but also in the collective. I realized then that the bond between human and spirit is indeed all encompassing within our space and time continuums, and yet we do not generally sense it in our sphere of material being. At that particular time and place, I gave intent for healing and manifesting my purpose, and it was not long after that my heart opened in accord and the messages flowed.

Personally I discovered, as expressed by Lee Caroll, "Anyone can channel, and Spirit is not proprietary in this regard. It's for all Humans, and not just a few. Therefore the ability and potential exists for this attribute for us all. Like so many other things, INTENT of the human means everything. Not all channelling is given with PURE INTENT. Therefore, some is real, and some is not . . . and YOU should be able to tell the difference when you HEAR or READ it. Is it really from Spirit?" Intent is the key, without fear it is a natural state, and it is definitely not new information. It has been around since the beginning times of Humanity on earth. It is not limited to sacred roles that only some people are enabled to do. Channeling is a process of opening ones perceptions to a higher capability, much like an artist or athlete when they are in the zone. It is power that emanates from within oneself, available for all and anyone who wishes to explore and learn the how of it. This is what I have found through my intent to begin, and uncover my own attribute for the role.

Message:

> *It is all so simple and yet you all complicate it with your ongoing search for something else. When are you going to dispel your fears and begin to trust in the real process of life, which is the unity of all entities on the planet? That is the real work that needs to commence. Not that of striving for this and that and chasing the ever elusive dream of material comfort. That will come as a natural extension of the love and warmth that you all share with your brotherhood.*
>
> *You are not islands dear ones, alone and floating on your own. You are all divinely connected through the essence of love that is the only truth that*

exists, now and forever. When you understand this simple law of life, then you shall come to realize that you are joined at the hip with your neighbours and then you shall also come to love them, as you learn to love yourselves.

There are so few who realize this simple truth and yet it is hidden only below the surface of your awareness and ready to jump to the forefront of your thoughts at any moment. You can all accomplish your goals and live in peace and goodwill, with a simple opening of the loving light that lies within each and every heart.

It is in goodness that lies the undoing of past hurts and pains. Once you realize that to give to each other is the source of all your happiness, it is then that the pain of isolation will be gone forever. You are all one with each other and therefore you need to understand that once you give up the search and start to simply give love to one another through comfort and consolation, then all else will be given unto you. This is the truth.

Be kind, caring, cooperative and above all else, respectful of each others right to live in love and freedom from the oppressions of hatred, scorn and tyranny. Let all live as one in harmony and create peace on earth. This is as it should be. Put aside your enmities and live in peace. The pleasures of life are simple and when you are in tune with the things you love to express, and in the company of family and friends you love, then your brightness will illuminate even the darkest places.

The change since the Industrial revolution and now the technology age has created busyness in people's lives. The need to accomplish and achieve in a physical sense instead of a spiritual sense has created a loss of awareness of simply being. Rushing here there and everywhere, people think they need to compete, to compare and be something other than who they really are.

The sense of self has become recognition with the external looks and has moved far away from the spiritual self, that people have lost sight of themselves. The "I am", is far removed and difficult to find. Be content with the simplest things for they are the richest. They are the things that touch your heart and will always sustain you in joy and happiness.

Inner Guidance:

Check in with your heart, at every turn in your life, and if it feels comforting, supporting, loving, then it is the way to go; to proceed through your life in such a state is the essence of your true being.

CHAPTER THREE

One with all

It all belongs to me

THE MORE I EXPERIENCED THE wonderful open-heart feeling and expansion of my being, I knew with certainty that I was attuned to and bonding with my innate wisdom. I sat excitedly each day, embracing my own unique talent to communicate and create with my highest self, rejoicing in the power emanating from the new awareness, my heart swelling in appreciation for receiving such stimulating messages. Within the beauty and simplicity of being, gradually I stepped more into owning my self-expression as a divine being, wholly trusting in the creativity manifesting so naturally through me. I felt my energy swell to encompass those connected feelings, and discerning the changes stirring within me, my outer world also shifted bringing clarity and a different view. My impression of the colours and energy vibrations of the trees, birds, sky, clouds and all surrounds my gaze fell upon, enlivened me. Feelings of absolute correlation with all life ushered in a sacred perception. I found communion with nature as a spontaneous extension of myself and understood that I was living with purpose and passion in each and every moment.

I recall a book I often read to my children when they were very young called, "My place in space"[3]. It was about undertaking an amazing journey into the far reaches of the universe. Beginning from your home, street and gradually expanding outwards, page-by-page building, from the city into the country, to other nations and then around the planet, and moving further into the vastness of the solar system. Then escalating even farther into the ever-expansive infinity of galaxies and space beyond. In any direction, wherever your imagination could take you. It certainly awakened my curiosity about the nature of living in the world, and understanding, astronomically, my place within it. I found it to be an ideal starting point for children, as well as adults, to begin to grasp the infinite wonders of life here on earth, as well as its expansiveness. The personal journey my children and I took was awesome, mind-boggling and humbling all at the same time, invoking many questions each contemplating the enormity of existence, and of being an integral part of it. It had offered me another perspective in which to see myself and where I fit within the bigger picture of all that is. Back then I had mentally glimpsed the link we all share within the framework of our physical reality.

Now I feel the emotional and spiritual connection from my heart and have first hand experience of knowing inherently who I am, recognizing myself as an energetic being of life. I know the capacity I have to be all I can be, simply because I exist in all things, am weaved into the very fabric of life and therefore an expression of its infinite power and beauty. I emphatically believed that I was living with purpose and passion and my relationships also began to reflect the changing effects of my unfolding self. I developed more tolerance in my communication with my partner Lee and in conversations I intently listened to his every word so that I could understand how he felt about the events and circumstances occurring in his world. He was my mirror, as I was his. Our lives ran parallel and I wanted to know him on a deeper level, so I could better know myself. What I discovered was that my goal to understand myself attracted all of the situations and people into my sphere to assist in the process. The link we all share, as one life force, naturally entitles and enables us to manifest the necessary components and players into our lives, which we require for our own self-transformation.

As a result of my intent, one of the struggles I have experienced throughout my relationships with men, relating to "being heard" began to shift. I had spent many agonizing hours stressing and mentally beating my self up in frustrated conflict with this old mindset and it was whilst attending a hilariously wonderful seminar conducted by Allan Pease[4] that I uncovered the source of this bone of contention within me. It was brought to my attention that biologically, men and women are so different with regard to listening, that as a woman, I should not take personally the fact that men are not that good at it, and I say this in all sincerity with tongue in cheek! Is it little wonder when they only need to speak about a quarter the amount of words daily that women do. This was a brilliant explanation for me, and one that I have a lot of fun with in banter with Lee and our female friends. It has certainly enabled me to lighten the load from my backpack of life patterns and beliefs and even though there are still times when I jump in to fight with my self over being heard, I now get over it very quickly and recognize the game for what it is, and the thoughts that can sweep me up in that mind battle.

Since then, I have also become very aware of listening to myself more and realizing that *I* needed to listen to me, rather than actually requiring anyone else to pay attention to me. By fully focusing on what others had to say, it also empowered my own aural functionality. I found stability and balance in this new course and at times in conversation, if I didn't sense I was being heard, I acknowledged the feelings of frustration I felt and immediately let them pass. I knew the issue was my own agenda and so no longer took it personally. It was such an enormous break through for me, lifting the veil and enabling me to hear my inner voice, resulting in such an astonishing flow of self-expression. In owning those old, uneasy emotions of self-doubt and insecurity, I had dived deeply into the association I share with *all* else, and the onset of self-mastery. I recognized how incredibly powerful I am in creating my world my way. I discovered that I am a piece of the puzzle of life, as is everyone and everything existent within the entire life cycle. Being in oneness, I know that everything reflected toward me, is of my own design. I give thanks for the opportunities that I receive from my interactions with all beings, be they human, animal or in spirit, who offer me a mirror into my self, allowing for continual transformation and growth.

Message:

> Being one with all is such an empowering feeling. The feelings of aliveness and vitality and the sense of being able to achieve anything, is stupendous and once you connect to the source of all creation, there are no limits to what you can be, do and have.
>
> The connection to the wonderful centre in your heart is so fulfilling. The energy that exudes from your being is timeless, zone-less and exists for

that purpose. Once you discover this place within is the source of all your creative activities, you realize the magnificence of aligning with its power, and you are set to sky-rocket your life to the moon, the stars and beyond. It is brilliant and transformative.

Breathe in the spaciousness and feel the energy flow through every cell in your body. Feel the peace and contentment in the moment with each breath. Freedom resides here and simply allowing your self to connect with your heart energy field, will stimulate the senses to stillness. In this place, fears and doubts do not reside, for they are only figments of the mind and once you connect to your higher energy, all negative energies fall away (do not exist). Expansion and awareness move through you and you recall "who" you really are; loving energy.

In stillness, you are one with all and can call to your conscious awareness, any being, teacher, and creative energy that are useful for your progress. Your connection with all empowers you to be all. The choices are multidimensional, and beyond the mental scope to perceive the reality. Limited in your progress and evolutionary cycle, individuals are opening their awareness channels to this reality and are now moving into greater freedom, love, joy and abundance, as is the plan.

The battles ensuing in the present earth time, are only a reflection of the egos attempt to maintain control of the human experience, before eventually letting go and releasing the soul to journey on as an enlightened being, living truly from the heart and divine energy source. For each one, the struggle will be of varying degrees depending on how much power the individual gives to the ego. Surrendering is the key to letting go and acknowledgement of the process. Recognizing and understanding the journey for what it is.

Once you have reconnected to your spirit at its core, a peaceful countenance is yours forever. You begin to live from there every moment of your life and in the knowledge of self you move in each moment with absolute faith, no matter what your life may appear on the outside.

In all things love shines a guiding light that beams a message of hope and inspiration. Be at ease with your self above all else. No one else exists except for your self, all else is an illusion and a double play, for we are at one ourselves and at one, we are all others too. Therefore, we are it all, in everything, all the time and therefore never alone. It is as it is. It is as simple as that. When we try to discover some other path, then we are lost. We have missed the point and our search is useless; we have headed into the darkness and are actually sailing away from port, rather than tying ourselves firmly to the moorings.

When you eventually turn inward to perceive this beauty and radiance, it is then that all who perceive you are also touched in the same way and then recognition of self is made apparent. They are the ones who will gradually walk through and begin the turning on of lights within each and every soul. It is the prophecy of ages that when this takes shape, then so too will the energy of the planet change and evolve and all things will come to pass that create the goodness that is meant to be.

We are all splendid and magnificent just as we are, and need no adornments. It is in this simple beauty that all shines so brightly and brilliantly. Take heart from this message because it means that we are never alone and forever have the companionship of those in all places, at all times, eternally. It is a blessing to know that we are never alone and that this state of ecstatic bliss goes forth forever. Never was there a more comforting note to receive than this, because it does away with fear and anxiety that our life will be terminated one day, by some inexplicable downfall of our bodies that carry us forth.

Recognizing yourself in all things simply means that you are already everything. How easy to manifest your desires when you know this simple truth. Be prepared to release and let go the old ways of thinking, to enable the greater goodness to flow through you.

Relax, for you are not alone in your journey and you are loved and supported abundantly in spirit.

Inner Guidance:

Every day, close your eyes for a few minutes, breath and relax into your body. Focus your mind on feeling the all-pervasive energy of aliveness within your heart as you breath in and exhale out. This simple process will enliven your senses, connecting you with oneness of being.

CHAPTER FOUR

All part of the plan

The plan is perfect, even when you think not, the plan is perfect

When I ponder my life, I realize that so many things that "happened" to me were all part of my unique life direction, and particularly, most of the events and circumstances occurred seemingly without my conscious awareness. Certainly, on occasions life appears to carry us along in a motion that is inevitable, and then at other times we come to a cross roads with a choice of decisions to make. From a purely conscious perspective this can be the way of it, however subconsciously there are also elements in play that deliberately shape the ground rules of our life. I now recognize those fundamentals as being tools for my spiritual unfolding, and a road map as part of my own distinctive design to know and expand my self, in all aspects of being. As with all of us human beings partaking in the game of life, we arrive here to experience the many challenges and consequent pains, so that we may appreciate, empathize and connect with each other compassionately. It is through specific plans, ones that we willingly chose to invite into our lives that enable each of us to learn the lessons needed, to awaken to the love that connects us all.

I remember as a young child, sitting around the dinner table, having wonderful and absorbing conversations with my parents about being adopted. At the age of eleven months, my birth mother had made the agonizing decision to place me up for adoption and the trauma I felt from the separation was locked deeply within me. I recollect feeling captivated when hearing the stories conveyed to me about the mother who had given birth to me, who lived out there in the world somewhere. I tried to picture what she looked like, and where she lived and what she did. I felt an aching chasm in my being along with an intense sense of curiosity to find her, see her and meet her. I needed to know who she was. I cannot even begin to describe the emotions I felt, it was all so surreal, and at that age in my life, I could not conceive in my mind how I would ever find her. I just knew that I would do whatever it took, some day, to locate her. I carried those thoughts with me constantly, like a hat glued to my head that I could never take off, and it seemed as if it was part of my extraordinary life plan.

I was totally and utterly intrigued by the conversations my adopted parents shared with me. What little they had been told, they related to me and I always remembered that my mother had come from an overseas country to live in Australia. She had been a seamstress, just like my adopted mum. The story at times seemed to be like a fairy tale of someone else's life and yet the circumstances of being adopted were one of the biggest triggers in my life. I cannot consciously recall ever asking for that situation to happen to me, but it did and it sent me on the search of a lifetime, a search for who I was. Many hurdles did I have to jump before I eventually came face to face with my "other mother", the one I had heard about for so many years and yearned to find. It was the impetus that sent me searching to ascertain and uncover the "I am" and it was a blessing in disguise. At times I felt desperate, and the empty ache in my body often felt so extreme I could barely endure it. The yearning to know; the need to know, were intense to say the least and they were all part of *my* plan, to walk through life and peel away the layers of emotional pain thereby exposing my sweet and gentle soul.

At the actual time of beginning my quest in earnest, I was very aware of the impact it could have on my adopted mother. She too had felt my pain of being taken from my birth mother, her own loss being when her mother had died when she had only been two years of age. Ushering me into her family, she had empathized with my grief and had poured out her heartfelt feelings to encompass me, providing me the love and comfort I sorely needed. She was like gold to me, and the last thing I wanted to do was to hurt her in any way. Being sensitive to her position was of the highest priority, and yet I had to communicate openly and honestly with her and this was confronting for us both. In our conversations we identified and discussed our fears and chose to step through them anyway, bridging the gap between us and building an even stronger bond than we already shared. In so doing we freed ourselves from the limiting patterns that would have held us tightly in grip had we not dared to challenge them.

During those years of searching, I began a new relationship and found my partner was also an adopted child. Not really surprising, as being mirrors for one another was part of our mutually arranged plan. We spent many hours phoning agencies, travelling interstate to speak with adoption groups and writing letters to government departments in our attempts to source the necessary breakthrough data. Because of the nature of adoption in those days, the doors of information did not open easily due to legislation and the task was exasperating at times. Having friends in high places lent a hand and my partner was able to secretly access records he needed to find his mother. I was not as fortunate, or at least I did not think so at the time. Persistently following a trail of facts I had gathered, I excitedly packed bags and optimistically headed interstate to stay with mum for a few days. This was the final stage in my search, I had done all I could and I wholeheartedly expected to receive the much longed for assistance I needed. Having exhausted all avenues I had tracked, I was now relying on others to hand over the goods. Bright and early the next day I could barely commute into the city fast enough, I was so sure that I would be given the news I longed for, the name of my mother.

There are times when our optimism is so strong that absolutely nothing can diminish the energy back of it. This was not one of those occasions. At every turn and with every person I spoke to on that day, my energy and enthusiasm became more and more deflated. From being on a high note, I plummeted into the abyss of misery. It was made quite clear to me, by several emotionally unattached persons, in bureaucratic places, that I would never, ever be able to find out the identity of my birth mother. It was simply the way it was, an actual fact, that my adoption orders had been closed, due to the date of processing. The legislation was never likely to change and so, sorry but you cannot know the longed for details you request. Feeling defeated and burdened with a heavy heart, I agonizingly departed the city a broken soul. I was in shock and wanted to cry out that it was unfair and how would you feel if it was you searching for your mother. I had traveled over eleven hundred kilometers just to be given that shattering news and I was completely devastated after hitting so many brick walls.

I had done everything I could. Doors that I thought would open easily for me did not and after much consoling from mum, I eventually decided to let go of the situation, and I returned home interstate. The night before I left, we spoke in length about our feelings and our desires to find her and we chose to let it be for the moment. If it were meant to happen it would have and we would take up the search again, another time. Very surprisingly a few days later, it was my adopted mother who was able to source what I had unsuccessfully yearned to find. Overjoyed and with tears flowing, she rang me to say she had felt a very strong urge to go and speak with the government agency herself. After explaining who she was whilst painting a picture of the situation, the woman she had spoken with had excused herself, gone into her office and shortly after returned with a small piece of paper that she inconspicuously slid across the counter. On the note was the name of a relative of my biological mother. In her wildest dreams, my mother had not expected that ever to happen and it knocked her for a six. Very kindly the lady, for unknown reasons, had chosen to step beyond her boundaries and assist us to open doors we could never have done on our own. For whatever grounds, she had risked her position to aid our plight. I had returned home, relinquishing my control over the events, leaving the task to a higher source, and was rewarded for my faith. To me, that was a miracle.

Shortly after, I met my biological mother and was deeply touched by her personal situation and the stories she relayed about her life. She expressed that many times she had also wondered where and how I was. It was so obviously apparent to me that part of our united plan, jointly scripted in another place and time, was to find each other again. As we reunited, gradually another chapter unfolded in both our lives, and the distance existent between us for all those years, began to diminish. Both she and my adopted mum became very good friends and I loved seeing them enjoying each other's company and being happy together. I found it was as important for me to know that they also shared a special bond, as I did with both of them.

Those were part of my special conditions, ones that I believe were created by me for my plan, in cooperation with my family both human and in spirit, which I came to earth to fulfill. They served me well in leading me to unravel my deepest pains and to consequently grow in alignment with greater self-understanding. It was through my immense desire to know more and to pursue it with the deepest conviction that eventually led to those doors opening. Without those events happening, my life would not be as carefree and happy as it now is and my heart would not be contentedly singing as it does now. The values of persistence, patience and holding unwavering faith were the mainstays of that amazing plan in action.

On embarking upon my investigations, I was met with many incredible and synchronistic events unfolding. It presented many opportunities for letting go of old baggage and allowing for unconditional love to flow between all of us participating in the plan. We each opened doors that perhaps we would never have considered otherwise, establishing new friendships and cementing old relationships. I learnt to trust and maintain faith in myself, as I trod life's inimitable roadway that leads to amazing grace. In reality those particular circumstances for me, were all about seeking my identity. They were all designed for my own spiritual development and growth, as part of my passage into self-awareness and insight. Those events were something that I had not consciously created to my knowledge at that time; however they were part of my life's plan and I am very grateful for the support I had both physically and spiritually along the way. I give eternal thanks for all that is and for being such an integral part of it.

Message:

The plan is beyond your scope of thinking (mind) and yet you also have the capacity to plot your course with free will. In allowing your mind the freedom to race away into the tomorrows or yesterdays, you lose the significance of the precious time you really exist within, which is the present, now.

It is in this perpetual place of being that all is uncovered and what you really seek is found. Tuning into your silent self and listening well with confidence and faith will guide you to each step you need to take in your life. With each small step a new door or pathway emerges for you to follow with agility and sure footedness.

You only have to slow the pace of your lives to feel the difference in your energies. It is a miracle of God that is so simple in its conception. There really is no need for hustle and bustle; it is the way you have created it with your thinking minds. The plan is to relax and enjoy your lush surroundings, to savour every glorious moment of breath and life. This is the simplicity of living fully.

You are not required to compete and to haggle and hassle; the plan in fact is just the opposite. It is not for you to question the plan, but merely play your part in it. It is an amazing dance of grace and wonder, and if you would observe the nature and beauty that surrounds you, you would but learn to follow the same sequence of steps.

We know of no other way to alert you to the precious nature of who you all are. You will not sit in quiet for long enough, to hear these precious words of wisdom within your own head, between your own ears. It is vital now, that this message is conveyed, for you are all needing to comprehend the nature of who you are, so that you can commence the journey of peace on this magnificent earth upon which you stand. It is the reason you all came to be standing exactly where you are. Do not fear this mission, as it is the inevitable truth of your existence in this realm of being. You are bound by your contracts to go forth and improve the land, reinstate it to its original glory.

And many of you are already spreading your wings in great consciousness of the job at hand. You love your work and stand in ceremony of the job you came to do. It will honour you greatly, that in courage you stand up and be noticed so that others will feel the call to express themselves in their chosen tasks.

With the newness of the energy and the messages there will be a gradual influx of souls who will attune to this information. The changes will not be apparent immediately but come as gradual stimulus, which can be easily and readily, absorbed into the energy patterns of the individuals. As with anything new it is a replacement of the old and as such takes time to incorporate into the very essence of all things.

You will observe these changes in the very places that need them the most; the education system, the political arena, the justice system, the hierarchy system. These systems must absorb the changes to pass onto the whole group of individuals.

When this happens there will be great upheavals as in any outmoded system. There will be downfalls and chaos before the new day lightens (emerges) bringing a total absence of the controlling factors that have until now been in place. A path of discovery for every soul is in order and there will be many joyful events that are harnessed in this new energy.

The benefits will be innumerable and the people will be well pleased. They will sing in the streets again and feel free to express on all levels of creation. The fears that so many carry in their substance will phase out and a renewal and splendour to be alive will prevail.

It is all worthy of the grandeur and greatness of the plan. The plan of life marches forward (or so you think), and yet is just as it is, at all times. In your human natures, you perceive it so differently than it really is and your comprehension of it all is so minute. If you knew the grandness, you would already be dancing in the streets.

If you can but open your self and see the entire picture of creation you would be bedazzled in such glory. And yet you do know this in your heart of hearts and in the recesses of your soul. The flames of life leap high and wide and in wonder you search your souls for the answers that you feel should appear in front of your eyes. And yet they will not, until you change the direction of your gaze. It is so simple really and yet you are all so conditioned by your training and learning that you have not been taught to look upon life in any other way.

There is no error, only correction and re-correction in the evolutionary process, repeated over and over again. This you know, so why fear, if you have been and done and known so many times before and once again here you be; what worry or concern is worthwhile within the plan. No need for any, except to align with the infinite loving energy and experience the joys and elations of life in each momentary experience.

At one and all the same for each and everyone, life exists to give pleasure and to receive abundance. In the giving is the overflowing love of renewal and regeneration. The spark of life is relit over and over and over again, ad infinitum.

Live in the moment; nothing else exists, nor really matters. Peace of mind dwells here. Feel your body vibrate to the rhythm of your spirit. Breathe in and release all tensions that have built up over time. Breathe it out and feel the release.

Be present at all times with yourself and you will know all of everything, and in this you will be lead to the richest life you could ever imagine, in synchronicity with life's enormous plan. Ignited by spirit you will fly to the four corners of existence and experience the most amazing journey you could possibly ever take; that of knowing yourself and all that you already are.

Fill yourself with the eternal life energy and enjoy a life of peace, love and absolute abundance. Never will there be a moment of pain, nor suffering, as you fly on the wings of divine love and soar to the heights of abandon. Have faith, let go the fears that keep you shackled and then the secrets of life will easily flow in almighty abundance. This is the plan. There is no other. With your free will you will be able to choose. One way is the death of self as you think you know it, the other way is the birth of who you really are. The choice is simple.

Primarily, the quest for knowing ones self is far from the minds of man, particularly because of the society in which most people are born into. However, it is an awakening process which has been sparked off now by the disorder in the outer world and the many difficulties that people are experiencing, at this time. This is happening on a greater scale now than ever before, as you recognize the plan and the game you play in it, and the illusion that is not the truth. And so in perfection, the plan is complete and you all walk in harmony and synchronicity with your own soul's calling, as is proper and in tune with the plan.

There is nothing that is not part of the plan and so all is well and in accordance with the plan. Take your selves (ego) out of the picture and instead replace it with a loving gratitude for each little thing and event that occurs in your lives. For it is not about you (ego) that is the most important, but about the evolution of the spirit, that which is the unseen factor and what you do not perceive through your physical being (external vision).

One must close ones eyes and stop looking "out there", and instead look within to see the magic of the moment. The wisdom of the ages attests to this and it is important to understand that there is no other way of "seeing" the truth. You have it back to front, do you not, and if you can simply reverse the way you look upon your lives, then you will see the abundance of life in its full regalia.

Be prepared to be surprised and then the inspiration will be born to discover that you are indeed all part of the amazing cosmos that is life itself. Plant your feet firmly within your inner being and you will never look back again. You will have found all the treasures that you could ever wish for to keep you contented and at peace, fulfilled and replenished.

Inner Guidance:

Be aware of your intuitive self. Begin to connect inwardly to read the energy and internal dialogue emanating from your soul being. We are all capable of tuning in, so begin now to listen to your own unique messages and be guided in each moment by your heartfelt self.

CHAPTER FIVE

In the stillness of the moment

In the stillness, shrieks the answers you yearn to hear

AT THE TIME OF RECEIVING these encouraging messages, my husband Lee and I were in the process of experiencing *extreme* financial hardship. I mean really depressive, devastating, living on the edge sort of dilemmas, ones that I am sure we came together to learn and grow from. We had initially *created* the money issues due to "pushing the envelope" too hard and yearning to have great financial wealth, *immediately* flowing into our lives. The sort of wealth that one wants now; the *instant gratification mind set* type of wealth. Instead what we yielded was as close as you can get to bankruptcy, and feeling totally out of control in our lives. We wanted change, and change is what we got, even though we had both brought material wealth into our relationship. I had been reading extensively about creating passive income for quite some time, so we chose to step beyond the *seeming* secure positions we held in the work place, and do something about following up on those ideas. Our thoughts attracted the exact vehicle for that very purpose.

We had followed a path of wanting to create abundance, of being financially free, with massive, passive income expected into our bank account regularly everyday. We attended seminars and were lured by the magic of the speakers we went along to hear about creating wildly wealthy amounts of money. We were told that if they could do it, so could we. Pumped up by the gloss and glamour, we stepped into the future, seeing ourselves already rich, even though we did not have the actual, physical money in our bank account. We read and heard that all you needed to do was to think rich and to see it already manifested, and so we did. Our error was in *assuming* that we would receive what we were creating with our thoughts, and then *spending* it before we actually had it. We were living our dream without actually having the means to do so in our pockets, and our credit card debt skyrocketed out of control.

Creating a real estate business at the time of the booming property market, we seized the opportunity to expand our knowledge, and using all of our accumulated resources we stepped into the arena and embarked upon the money making game. At the time, we discovered a system whereby if we assisted other people to purchase their dream home, then we would also be helping ourselves to great profits. A great concept and one that does well in certain markets, creating a win, win situation for all parties involved. For us the timing was perfect for the challenges that were to appear in our lives. We were right in the midst of the economic downturn, interest rates rising and a change in market conditions. The shift created the effect of placing most people's affordability and serviceability at risk, radically altering the whole scenario and leaving us in a precarious position.

Profits made from the business were used to tenuously keep it running, and we attended more workshops and seminars on "how to be rich, just like the richest people in the world" in an effort to learn more techniques, *hoping* to work our way out of trouble. We even extended ourselves further into more massive credit card debt to keep afloat, convinced that our efforts would succeed in the end, and being hyped up by the possibility that one day, *in the future*, we would also be successful, just like the people whose seminars we attended. Even though we had gleaned a great deal of very positive information throughout our learning experiences, we were not mentally, nor emotionally equipped for the negative downside of a changing property market. Nor did we understand fully the actions required for building wealth and more importantly, keeping it. Our mindsets were not wired sufficiently to maintain what we created. We were in over our heads.

Our situation became critical and we searched desperately for other ways to alleviate the negative financial hole we found ourselves in. We learnt about buying and selling on ebay, we attended more seminars, believing more facts and figures would help our situation, when in fact we just got more into arrears as we stood on the edge of the cliff. In exasperation, we began selling off cassette tapes and books we'd purchased at seminars, as well as personal belongings just to get a few bucks to keep us ahead and able to pay the onslaught of bills that would not subside. With insufficient cash flow we were in big trouble, having put all our money into making money. Desperately we *tried* to make things come together, wanting to reestablish the circumstances around us that would make the purse strings balance. We needed money urgently and *tried* to get finance to buy a local business because we thought it would be the answer to our prayers. Surely then we'd be able to get ourselves back on track with money flowing into our lives rather than out, and be able to work our way out of debt. Our attempts with lenders fell short however and we seemed *stuck* and unable to physically *fix up* our problems. Our minds were constantly thinking of things to do that would help the disastrous situation we found ourselves in.

In utter urgency, we also borrowed money from our closest friends and family, all with good intent at the time to repay them within a short period of time. Things got tighter and tighter, and the more we *tried*, the deeper hole we dug for ourselves. Constant and extreme feelings of anxiety were unbelievable and at times it seemed a better idea to end it all then and there, rather than have to continue going through the dire motion of not knowing what to do or how to free ourselves from such a gigantic financial hole. Emotions were continually surfacing of fear and guilt and a huge sense of helplessness. When I thought of previous issues I had experienced during my life, in comparison with these ones, they felt very meager indeed. Being so pummeled by our circumstances, we felt as if we had lost all sense of hope and freedom.

Our saving grace was our continuing faith, knowing the challenges we faced were of our own making. We had deliberately gone into debt to have what we perceived would be a better life than we already had. We thought we wanted more than what we already had, materially speaking, and thinking that it would enhance our lives and make us happier. We wanted the big bucks, not only for ourselves, but also to help our family, and we thought several million dollars should do it. It was as if we were in the midst of learning the most mammoth lesson around money that one could ever imagine, and particularly, the way in which we *thought* about having it. We discovered that what you resist will persist, and the harder we tried to get ourselves out of the conundrum, the more we actually got into debt.

The idea of being *financially wealthy* soon became very stale, and our only concern was surviving, and somehow getting the creditors off our backs. More than anything, we wanted to stop the persistent and ongoing phone calls demanding we catch up and pay our dues. The feelings of apprehension and frustration, of not knowing how to, would often bring us to our knees, the sense of helplessness overpowering us.

We could have easily collapsed into a big heap, terrified of the outcome. Facing the thought of bankruptcy was the final frontier and I decided to look it squarely in the face. Why not dare challenge my most fearful thoughts. In those moments, I realized that nothing could *ever* happen to me that would not bring the next day dawning into my life. I knew then that the *entire experience* Lee and I were caught up in, was really about growing in self-awareness and understanding. It was all about our beliefs and specifically about our money consciousness, or lack of it. I felt very humble indeed, most of the time and gradually began to step back mentally from hooking my emotions into the situation. Meditation became my best friend, stilling my mind and enabling me to stay present, keeping my spirits high and continuing to maintain self-confidence.

We learnt to deal with events when and as they occurred. We knew that what was happening in our lives was purposeful, and we also realized that to keep balance and sanity, we needed to live positively in each moment. By practicing daily to still the rampant thoughts of insecurity constantly surfacing, we came to recognize that *in the moment, there is nothing to fear*. We chose to stay with the discomfort and accept the challenge for what it was. By stilling the mind and tuning inwardly to the quiet voice of spirit, the God within, the situation became bearable. It was in those moments that the beautiful messages flowed so easily and became a constant source of strength and inspiration to me. Never before had I enjoyed the connection with my higher being as I did then, and continue to do so. There is a saying that you can never go back, and that was how I felt as I moved each day through that unbearable state of affairs.

It was not long before we found ourselves in the position of having to leave our home, a beautiful two storey Mediterranean style house, commanding magnificent ocean views, located in a quaint seaside village. Even though we rented the house, we really loved it and the location, and had always aspired to owning it one day. It was one of our big dreams. Being notified of a rental increase was the trigger event we needed to reassess our financial situation, knowing we could no longer afford to live there. It was time to *let it all go*, and move forward into unknown territory. Once we had made the decision to move, "to God knows where", we felt a great sense of freedom and relief, along with a sense that everything would be all right for us. Holding on to something that we had no control over was futile and so we stored our belongings and with faith in our hearts, we headed down an uncertain track, and for a while we visited family in Adelaide. At least we had no rent to pay, and the bills accruing on the back burner could wait a little longer. We were venturing into pastures new and it felt exhilarating in a funny sort of way. In the middle of chaos and uncertainty, we held the light. We had a brief reprieve from having to think about anything.

Returning a few weeks later, we began to ask ourselves which direction to take and where could our new home be? Feeling a mix of uncertainty mingled with a sense of excitement of the unknown, it was as if we were being guided, every step of the way, without struggle. Trusting the process completely we received so much support from our family and friends, and when asked where we were going to live and what were we going to do, we had absolutely no idea. We had pinned some hopes on winning a lottery prize home, and that did not eventuate. Talk about wishful thinking! It was about a week later, when an astonishing array of synchronistic events began to play out for us. We received messages regarding moving north to Queensland and so we followed the trail. Lee searched the Internet and checked availability of rental properties. At the exact same time, I was chatting with my daughter and her partner and they mentioned an area that we had briefly visited for an anniversary treat a year or so earlier. We had been drawn to the location for its sheer beauty, so why not check it out. When I returned to make the suggestion to Lee, he had also seen a property for rent in the very same location and had already phoned the agent to enquire if it was still available.

I was stunned, the doors began opening. The next day we visited the realty office, were given directions and found a workman doing repairs at the house. It was perfect, a lovely little cottage, and exactly right for our Lucky dog and us. It was in a beautiful tree lined, peaceful street and it was reasonably priced within our means. When we returned to talk with the property manager, she told us there had already been several other people interested in letting the house. One couple had taken the lease agreement to sign and then unexpectedly returned it having changed their minds. We were asked to fill out an enquiry form if we wanted to proceed with the application, and as our belongings were packed away several hours drive in another state, we could not easily access documents to verify ourselves. Surprisingly, the agent simply asked for phone numbers of two contacts that she could call as referees on our behalf. In the meantime, we went for some lunch while they did the check and during our meal we received the phone call to confirm that we could go ahead and rent the house if we wanted it. Talk about proceedings availing themselves so positively and effortlessly, I could still not believe it. We were thoroughly astounded at the uncomplicated nature of how from moment to moment our lives were changing, and we felt somewhat stunned and very, very grateful.

We returned a week later, possessions in tow and stepped into our new home. The agent told us that since our decision to take up the lease, there had been several more enquiries to let the property but we knew it had been ear marked for us. By then we were not at all surprised, for we had let go mentally of ascribing to every detail of our functioning, instead remaining content in the present with what we had and listening for the directives to flow into our conscious awareness. Being guided to take the steps necessary for all our needs to be met. Having made a firm decision to move on, we had channeled that data to our subconscious mind, our soul self, who had then taken the reins to steer us to our next port of call. Our hearts opened wider with unquestioning resignation, and even though we were still digging our way out of the financial bog we had shaped for ourselves, we recognized the turning of another corner. With our intention to broaden our awareness in each moment, we knew we were in the right place, at the right time, doing the right thing.

Message:

> The human who can develop stillness, will lead the way in the expansion of the consciousness of being. The continued practice of being still will enable the mind to take a place in the quiet back alleys of the higher self. Then and there you observe your mind (ego) in the process of daily chatter and communication of the type that keeps the self busy and bustling to achieve in the external world.

On observation, one can then practice the process of returning to stillness and of being in the moment. Be prepared for an initial battle with the logical mind, because it has run the show, literally, in your life for many years. It will resist the change and it is at these times that you must be present to "see" and to return to being still in the moment.

Doors open in mysterious ways and they are beginning to do that for you. Continue to be still and live in each moment energetically, holding absolute faith in the direction of your life. Life is lived now and nowhere else. Maintain your goals and stay firm and committed. Allow the developments that take shape; be in synchronicity then with your momentary activities. You do not need to feel anxious or think that there is more to do; the path is clearly set and it is in the moment that events take their natural course.

Enjoy every moment and then you will truly feel fulfilled instead of "wishing for" some other futuristic plan to develop. Have fun and live joyfully, in each moment. Once you take yourself off the path of being in the moment, you can lose yourself to all the overwhelming thought patterns thrown at you, by your ego. It is in the stillness of the moment that God speaks and reminds us of our sacred natures. In that place, all is well.

When you feel anxious, confused, or distressed by some event or circumstance, the best remedy is to be found in the stillness of the moment. All is released to spirit who reconnects, and then allows for solution to pass through you in truth. Faith is the nourishment of spirit. When all seems amiss, or when a pain persists, the healing is to be found in communion with spirit.

Treasures are unlimited, growth is unlimited; when one knows oneself truly and trusts that life is the fuel of worth and abundance in every scenario, then one can continue on the path with full realization that support and love are always at hand from spiritual dependence.

When you know this in your very soul and being, then everything is always all right. There is never a moment needed to be spent in fear or concern. The flow of your life will harmonize with spirit and provide you with all your needs and desires. This will happen in easy flow, with no apparent effort or struggle. You will have put your faith totally in the presence of love, which is your essence and that which exists in every moment.

Grace and gratitude flow through you, and then you really are alive and in synchronicity with the God within. In this, is great beauty and bounty and you shall shine your light upon the earth, to all with whom you touch. The struggle ends there, and the real power of purpose ignites you towards your desired direction, and to achieve your greatest ambitions.

Stay focused and clear, and ever positive. Be spontaneous in all your actions, never hesitating to flow in the direction that each moment takes you. It is in the moments that life exists, and in no other place. In stillness all is revealed and revered. The lessons of life are heard in this silent space.

Time is of no consequence in the plan of life when lived in the moment. Satisfaction comes from staying centered in peace and joy, and existing in the now. Problems do not exist in this state and also with this new perception comes relaxation and awareness of ease and going with the flow of life, rather than the need to mentally figure everything out. In this state of relaxed awareness, answers are channeled from a higher source.

This is the challenge, to be still. In this peaceful place, one finds the toolbox; the strength, the support, the love, the family and the secrets that unfold a life of extraordinary quality and fun. One must trust, that is all, and totally surrender. Letting go of preconceived ideas and outcomes is crucial to this simple activity. Creating time to sit in quiet is necessary.

You must be still and cease to be so concerned. All is well and it will always be so. It is just a case of self-trust, instead of self-sabotage. You are the creator and therefore have the power to build anything. You have no idea until you let it all go. Focus only in the moment and do not let anything distract you from your higher purpose. This is the lesson. Things will resolve themselves when you take the necessary action steps towards that resolution.

Be still and know I am God. Make the reconnection without any other thought attached. No need to strive or try; no need to harp on any other particular practice, only the true one that carries you swiftly to your divine core. In time this process is so natural that one can be in this state of oneness with self at all times, in all situations, thus radiating such peace, love and harmony to all other fellow beings.

Inner Guidance:

Stillness is an integral part of who you are. Connect daily to the quietness of life, through walks in nature, along the beach; be alone with your self. In your mind step back and become aware of your thoughts and your reactions to them. Be the quiet observer.

CHAPTER SIX

Surrendering

Walk your path in surrender to your own heart's calling

HAD I NOT REACHED THE unenviable position I found myself in financially, I would perhaps still be playing out my old and regular mind dramas. However, my spirit has always had different plans for me other than those that stem from my ego and everyday thoughts. Now in my life, I find at the very time that I am most vulnerable to falling over (so to speak) through my present economic circumstances, is the most opportune time to trust myself implicitly and listen to my quiet inner whisperings. In this loving space, I have put my absolute faith in living true to my heart and appreciate the quality of such a union.

In a physical sense, at any moment it seems that I am about to fall off the planet, so disastrous things can appear, particularly in a monetary sense. However, in terms of being still and knowing there exists a much grander plan that I cannot always perceive, I have placed an unwavering conviction. Rather than trying to chart an outcome from my anxious thoughts alone, I defer to a superior source of direction that assures me, in my heart, that all is well. And as I warmly bask in this reality, I fall deeper and deeper into a surrendered state of tranquility and self-assurance. If this will help the unfolding of my erratic life production, only time will tell. However, I have an inkling that it is one of the most significant aspects of being who I am. In this alert state I feel the expansion of self as I succumb my life circumstances to my higher celestial being, 'to take on board' knowing that I, in my smaller state of mind, could not possibly fathom.

In permitting myself to let go of my "external" problems, I detect a sense of protection running through me from a higher presence, the silent partner that I am, being in full throttle of the outcome and therefore feeling not the slightest amount of fear. In relaxing and listening, being aware of the ever-present signs and symbols that are offered up in every moment, there exists only the potential to resolve any issue, without struggle or fear. Within the challenge, lies the solution. Materially, sometimes I have absolutely no idea how I am going to be able to make ends meet. Yet always a light turns on, a message comes and I follow the prompt, and my every need is supplied by utilizing what I have available in that moment. Those possessions stockpiled, waiting for relief, are dealt with in the natural course of each moment, and as my perception shifts, so does the illusion of a problem, which is seen only through the eyes of scarcity thinking and a fabrication of the mind.

One of the many lessons I have had the privilege to experience, is learning to laugh in the face of adversity. One particular task that most of us experience regularly involves food shopping. I would often wonder, with the little money I had available at times, how I was going to buy groceries for an entire week. I would front up to the supermarket with a list I had written, of a carefully organized menu, and search out the items I needed which were on special. I treated it as a game, one that I decided to have fun with. I would laugh at myself as I wandered the aisles, adding up the items I had gathered, not wanting to spend more than my meager budget allowed. Amazing grace and gratitude was an integral part of the pastime and I was always surprised that at the end of shopping, I had sufficient supplies to meet our needs. *I can have fun, fun and more fun when shopping* became my mantra.

When I first began playing the shopping game, it was anything but fun. I would be acutely stressed about having inadequate means with which to buy the food items. My feelings would run rampantly out of control. Why is this happening to me? Poor me, how am I going to make ends meet? I would almost be in tears with the frustrating emotions I felt. My mind would have a field day with my feelings, playing havoc at every possible opportunity. And then I would stop, breath deeply several times, and stay myself in the moment, feeling the depletion of the situation. The scenario enabled me to develop control and self-reliance, not through panicking and acting irrationally, but by listening intently to my intuitive voice. It was the quiet resonance of spirit that stilled the thoughts and emotions, bringing assurance and comfort that all was well.

Now I thoroughly enjoy shopping for every single item and I am grateful to have the opportunity to purchase food at all. Feeling enjoyment from choosing wisely, guided by my wallet, actually has served the purpose of letting go of *have to and should*. I always trust that I will be able to put food, of good quality, on my table for our enjoyment, and I always can. My appreciation for being supported no matter what my circumstances has escalated. I know that life serves me always, and learning to surrender and accept, instead of struggle, has been a massive journey in humility. My conversations with self are now positive affirmations of pleasurable and abundant living. I have learnt that having a moderate amount to spend is essentially enough most of the time and again it is about the beliefs one carries within them that make the world of difference. I am truly blessed when I look around me and witness the beautiful environment in which I live, the peacefulness, yet expansive view my life encompasses. Surrendering to my circumstances has aided in adding everything I could possibly need. I now know that I am abundance, and it is so, and that money is just another tool from which to learn this most important lesson.

When we take departure of our external concerns and align with our inner guidance to assist us through the calamities and catastrophes, then our roads are less strewn with debris and we begin to step our way safely and surely in the direction led by our hearts instead of our heads. This can clear our mind of finding a solution and opens ourselves to the enjoyable moments of being, which can bring peace and resolution in that quiet and protected place. Time is of no consequence in the plan of life when lived in the moment. Satisfaction comes from staying centered in balance and harmony, and existing in the present. Problems lessen with a change of perception, and the need to mentally figure everything out shifts to a much more relaxed attentiveness. In this state of calm alertness, answers are channeled from a higher source, with the ability to embrace the challenges, knowing that each and every circumstance is an opportunity for our growing awareness.

Message:

Surrendering to your mission and aligning with your higher self in accomplishing the goals you came to earth to achieve and living true to your hearts desires you are now embarking upon your chosen path.

Spirit guides you to your best options, easily and effortlessly and in this you must trust. You step to the next rung of the ladder each time you surrender your thoughts to the guidance of your higher self. This takes practice because the eager ego is quick to convince you otherwise.

In actual fact, once we find our true essence is spirit and infinite (never dies), our lives take on a new and exciting dimension. We can surrender and enjoy the quality of living fully present in each moment, not being too absorbed in the dilemmas of the physical realm. We can live from spirit with self-assurance on our path through life and address the physical concerns when and if they present a challenge.

You've made mistakes, forgive your self; you are now in correction mode. You are not alone, and you are definitely not in any mind set issue over these concerns. The righting is occurring in each moment, as you know. Have faith that all is well and take the steps in each moment to resolve the issues. Be only responsible for your input and no one else's. The web you weave in thoughts is not a place for solution. Only in quiet will the light go on and reveal the answers that you need.

Just let it all go. As you practice surrendering, you will find that all solutions appear without effort. You will stop struggling and allow for divine energy to bring you what you need. It is this simple.

When you feel your mind take over, be aware of the sensations this brings to your body. Immediately process these negative thoughts, as they will not help you, or aid your situation. One of the reasons you have the issues on your plate, is so you may be able to test and try the ways of solution through spiritual inspiration, versus the ego. Without the trial and test, how is one to discover the correct elucidation.

Allow your body to relax fully and then enjoy the peace this brings. Allow yourself to be supported by spirit and you will then feel the surrender this brings. Stay in awareness at all times, in every moment, for this is the answer.

Amazing options will appear, when you least expect them to. Doors will divinely open and you shall be totally supported in the moment, with each and every situation.

You yourself are the catalyst for the changes in your life and the incredible miracles that will appear. Be sure that you know it is no other than your self who triggers these events, so trust your self. When you open to the divine loving essence that is your true identity, the most amazing events take place.

You have no idea until you let it all go. Your higher self then takes the reins and guides you to the most wondrous places. Do not rush anything; take your time. In surrendering, the way will be lit by spirit for you to travel your path, well blessed with everything you desire, without fear or worry, or anxiety of it being fulfilled.

Surrendering and letting go is the key. The saying "get out of your own way" is the perfect statement that exemplifies this process. When you let go, it is then that the unseen forces of life carry you to new levels of experience and it is then that your passions and desires become reality in your outer world.

Take heart, for this is just the beginning. When more and more beings start to embrace these living concepts, then life on the outside will take on enormous transformation. You will all benefit from the goodness that life supplies so naturally and then peace and joy, and goodwill amongst all mankind will exist in perfect harmony.

Healing happens in every aspect of our lives when we let go of the need to control the outcome. By surrendering to our higher source of energy to complete the task, or healing process, we flow in synchronicity with divine energy and embrace the healing fully, without preconceived thoughts of how it "should" happen.

When we let go, even greater gifts are given and more than we could ever imagine happens in our lives. We are expanding into the greater wisdom of life and flowing harmoniously.

As you expand to new heights of consciousness, your sense of peace and happiness and acceptance lifts. You no longer fight with your self on the old level of understanding and instead easily accept the challenges, feel the emotion and allow the stillness of your higher being to direct your course of action. This is surrender and support.

In all things life unfolds perfectly and when the ego is displaced by the easy flow of understanding and recognition, then events flow naturally to the releasing state of no-longer-needed resistance.

All is well, in every moment

Inner Guidance:

Become conscious of your mental hold on life and how it unfolds daily. Let go, let go, let go and know the peace of trusting your higher self to guide your way. Communicate with your spiritual self through meditation and visualization. Feel your heart's vibration as you step into knowing yourself on a deeper level.

CHAPTER SEVEN

Live courageously

Have the courage to live the life you deserve and embrace the challenges

THERE IS SO MUCH LOVE in the world and we are never alone, and this is how I see my life now. So often when we are striving to please others we lose sight of this reality and get caught up in our own mental ostracism which leads us further into beating our self into a small, insecure state of being. My own personal observation of this practice has helped me enormously to break free from such limiting mind games. Generally, we live our lives from so many unperceived, conditioned patterns of accepted behaviour, having never been taught how to question those beliefs through self-exploration and examination, often feeling very disempowered and unfulfilled. We fear uncovering those layers of so called emotional security because they tie us to our beliefs so strongly. Who would we be without them?

From a young age we have learnt to place such high expectations on achieving at some level, whether it be academically or at sport for instance. In some way, we regard ourselves *as* the accomplishment and when we push too hard and do not fulfill the deed or event, or live up to the expectation, we chastise our self in the worst possible way. This then opens the door to feelings of inadequacy, anger, guilt, frustration, to name a few, and a sense of not only letting our self down but others as well. We then tend to also, without conscious awareness, transfer those feelings and thoughts onto the people around us whom we love, particularly if we do not take the responsibility for owning our own feelings. At this point we are on a merry-go-round of emotional dysfunction and we have not learnt how to step off it and look within ourselves for the answers. Blaming other people for our lot in life seems much easier than being accountable for changing it our self.

This is what happened to me shortly after I had met my birth mother. I was very mindful of being in a child like state, feeling innocent and needy. She was after all the mother who had carried me within her and given me life, and even though she had not raised me as her infant, I still felt the strong bond between mother and daughter and placed her on that maternal pedestal. Her family had opened their home and hearts to me, and I felt quite fragile stepping into that arena, still feeling my way through the complex emotions I was experiencing. In finding my mother, I had also uncovered an entirely new lineage including brother and sister, and I felt exposed somehow, as if all eyes were on me. Gradually getting to know each other, progressively over a few years, it became increasingly apparent to me that I could only be known to my mother's friends as an acquaintance, occasionally visiting her from out of town. For her own private reasons, I was unable to be acknowledged for whom I was in her life, her biological child, and this felt extremely difficult for me to accept. It did not sit well for me at all, particularly after searching inwardly as an adolescent and then outwardly as an adult, until I finally found her.

I could not easily come to terms with her behaviour and I felt, once again, a sense of abandonment. In my dreams of being with her, I had believed that she would readily accept me as one of her children. In that state of mind, it had never occurred to me that my appearance in her life might unbalance and threaten her sense of established security. I battled with myself for a long time, rejecting the idea. I desperately wanted to feel part of her family, wholly and solely. Belonging to a family unit was primary for me then, and suddenly I was confronted with the old familiar feelings that I carried, crying out for recognition and identity. Having counseling at the same time to help my marriage added fuel to the already burning fire within me, and I found myself in a very dark place, confused and bewildered. My issue was that I felt my identity hinged on my mother's ability to tell everyone in her life who I was. Then I would be emotionally stable, and attribute myself as the child of the mother that I had always hoped for, making me who I was.

Slowly I began to realize the futility in my need to be recognized and I became angry with my mother and wanted to blame her for my inadequacies. I started to question who I was and fell over badly within myself, not understanding at the time that I was relying on someone outside of myself to prop me up. I deeply related with the fear of letting go of the emotional dependency I had held onto for years, to protect myself from the pain. My heart ached and the long time feelings of rejection that I had carried within me began to surface. I came face to face with the horror of the situation as a young child being given away, and I confronted the hidden pain, deeply embedded within my being. The disturbing outburst I felt was like a wild beast bellowing as it goes to slaughter and the release of pain was like nothing I had ever known before. The long held onto aching wounds began to surface, creating spasms of emotional release freeing me at last. I immediately felt tremendous relief from years of mentally glossing over a situation in my life that I had thought I had no control over. Now I realized it was *entirely* up to me to change those aspects that I did not like. It was I who had the power to change myself.

Part of my healing was to convey to my mother how I really felt about the situation, so I wrote her a letter. Through the counseling that I was undergoing and the steps I was taking to understand myself, I was able to be *impeccable with my word*5 by telling her exactly how I was feeling. More than anything, I wanted to start being true to myself, to stop playing it safe, and step into being responsible for owning everything I felt. I wanted to live from my heart and not from the fearful thoughts feeding me from an old belief. I realized that I no longer needed something from my mother to make me the person I was and that felt good, very, very good, as I stepped into my own power. I was very aware that she may not comprehend and I chose to take the risk. I had to do it for me, and I also knew that we could work through whatever arose from my actions. When we next met up, we communicated openly and the true healing began between us. My acquiescence of the situation served to highlight my own acceptability and from then on I was on the brilliant road to trusting me.

In her way, she had shone a light upon my darkness and given me an incredible opportunity to grow internally, and I am so grateful. Through those years when we were feeling our way we each other, our relationship was sometimes strained, and yet always, there abided a loveable bond between us. I was still growing up myself, and eventually it was when I gave birth to my own children, that I began to understand how parenting plays such an integral and amazing part in discovering more of ourselves. I suddenly woke up to how difficult my mother's life had been and how much suppressed pain she had carried within her, for so many years. I learnt about compassion and the meaning of caring for those we love, unconditionally. We now share a loving, open relationship from a distance and we are only a phone call away. When we get together the love flows abundantly and we are wonderful friends, sharing beautiful moments that are very pleasurable. I appreciate more than ever the chance I was given, and chose for myself, to discover the greater part of me, through the painful lesson of being an adopted child. I would not change anything about the incredible journey it took me on. I braved the unknown in search of fulfilling a deep inner need, not knowing where it would lead. Courage and determination were my guides.

Message:

Be friends with yourself, at all costs, you do not need to be battling your self first. With kindness in your heart, goodness flows and harmony prevails. There is no space for any other emotion to dwell. Peace then prevails in perfect unison within each soul, touched by the presence of love and goodwill.

In every situation and circumstance, no matter how negative, there is also the opportunity for goodness and greatness. It befits us all to change our view of the world and to really see the mystery and the greatness of everlasting life. Discard your blinkers and look anew at the wonders of the world.

Fear is the illusion of life. It stops you in your tracks and keeps you small and frail. Instead of spreading those glorious wings and heading into the thermals to the heights of creating what you all want you stay on the ground with your tired feet firmly anchored in your self sabotaging fears. You do yourselves such an injustice. This one thing alone stops your progress and does not allow for the natural flow of trust and love that binds you all.

The flames of life leap high and wide and in wonder you search your souls for the answers that you feel should appear in front of your eyes. And yet they will not, until you change the direction of your gaze. It is so simple really and yet you are all so conditioned by your training and learning that you have not been taught to look upon life in any other way.

When we take departure of our external concerns and align with our inner guidance to assist us through the calamities and catastrophes, then our roads are less strewn with debris and we begin to step our way safely and surely in the direction led by our hearts and not just our heads.

Be at peace with your brothers, all over the world. The history books tell the age old tales of battles and defeats, of deaths and tragedies and yet this is all man made, yet done in the name of God. How can this be true and so? God's name is only used as a word described by your very selves; your real God spirit and ally consists of the loving light of existence. It is not in God's name that battles are fought, but in man's supremacy to be the best, to beat him self up, in truth.

For he only does this to himself. He alone battles with him self. He really only plays the game alone. And so it is in every situation and crisis that man continues to beat his brains out, trying to solve his (mans') issues and problems. If he but understood that he has bypassed the very essence that dwells within him that could be of greatest assistance. There are no battles to fight (and win), only the surrender of all things to his own loving source, to shine and heal every situation that exists in his life.

How simple this is. It but takes a slow down in the pace of his affairs and real centered concentration and connection with his inner being, his higher self. The lesson is easy and yet frightens the hell out of most men. To take stock and slow down and to even consider the simplicity is such a big deal. When this happens though, the riches that appear are worth the efforts. And efforts they are truly not, but just a simple practice of stilling oneself for long enough, getting uncomfortable and really settling into that most wonderful, peaceful state of rest.

In this blissful state, one will discover the answers to illness, the directions for problem solving, with such ease that it is miraculous. It is the wonder and truth of life and the connection each and every one has with self (the God self) within. It is a practice, done anywhere and at anytime; no need for any shrines, halls or ceremonies; it can be a simple case of pausing one's thoughts and reconnecting in the moment to the ever abiding stillness within.

Simple, simple, simple, this is the truth. No need for science books, history books, any books in fact. Once the habit of practicing self awareness occurs, the process is etched in the memories and is easily accessed when the need or desire takes hold in any moment. This is the truth of enlightenment.

Live your birthright; this is who you are. A work of divine art, displaying your love and light upon the earth, bringing treasures to all others in your sphere and along your path.

Take time to listen and share with another. You have all the time in the world. If you can but uplift another's spirit, then you have done your work. This is the key, to find the peace within and you will discover the peace without.

Enlightened beings one and all, you need no other practice except to return to your hearts and live from that state of everlasting love, which dwells in waiting and ever present abundance, and self acceptance of the truth. Have the courage to live the life you deserve. Risk it all in pursuit of the dream of love, which is itself you. When you love, then love you are, and all else comes together.

Celebrate the challenges and embark upon the learning as if it was a new experience in each moment, as a child would do as he learns to walk and step through the stages of human (physical) development. This is as it is, every step of the way through life, for adults do not stop growing, if physically, then certainly not mentally, emotionally and spiritually. They only "think" they do. Arrival never, ever happens, and this is the wonderment and excitement of "being" alive, and life itself "being".

Inner Guidance:

It becomes a king to act kingly and to honour all in his kingdom. Take the time daily to listen to what other people have to say. Focus your energy on brightening another beings moment, a smile will do, or a stop for a chat. This can make their day, and certainly it will uplift your own.

CHAPTER EIGHT

Accepting responsibility

You are the only one responsible, there is no other

TAKING RESPONSIBILITY FOR *ABSOLUTELY EVERYTHING* that happens in our lives is perhaps the hardest thing to do. Sometimes it seems a lot easier to point the finger at someone else for the problems you face, or to blame another for your circumstances. As previously mentioned, from my past history I have found it to be a very disempowering place to live, and yet to be responsible for your actions can also feel threatening to your overall sense of security. It can disrupt old patterns and beliefs that have been so tightly held onto for much of ones life. It takes courage and an about face in your awareness, along with a conscious intention to change those things which no longer serve you well. It also means accepting the consequences of your actions and choices in life. From what I have learnt, responsibility is having the *ability to act* rather than react to situations.

Quite often as a result of our earlier experiences growing up, when our parents and teachers admonished us, along with the odd friend or two, we tended, generally unconsciously, to become defensive of the harsh and abrasive handouts given. Without ever realizing, we formed various behaviour modes as protective armour, creating insulation from abuse. At an early age whilst establishing our unique identity and place in the world, we decided subconsciously to act in the very same ways as we had been treated, creating the buffer necessary to survive the painful onslaughts. Those learnt patterns became our padding against further hurts and we simply shelved the feelings such as guilt, fear and shame deeply within our core being, easily justifying our own actions, because the same thing had happened to us, by the people we loved and respected. In this way those beliefs were reinforced and aided excusing our codes of conduct.

With unawareness, we continue to support dysfunctional patterns of behaviour, and deny our intuitive faculties that can play a part in determining our consequential (response) (able) action. Made even more difficult at times because of peer pressure and an emotional need to be accepted by our cohorts. On a subconscious level, we create blocks to feeling our painful emotions and simply learn to live life from those embedded beliefs. That then becomes the habitual system in which we survive as we grow up. Instead of learning to honour our instincts and to listen to our hearts, we allow our ego to dictate the terms of our livelihood, playing out the same-recorded communication that we had unconsciously programmed at a much earlier age. We are rarely taught to pay attention to and recognize our angry and frustrated outbursts and therefore be responsible for our words and deeds that may follow. We remain playing the same small mind games that kept us relatively safe and comfortable, at the same time hindering us from learning, and bringing to the forefront of our mind, ways to deal with those imprisoned emotions. Without awareness, we become either the victim or the victimizer. We do not learn to *think about how we are thinking*, and generally not to *feel how we are feeling*. Angry feelings block the pain and the initial reaction is to strike out and hurt someone or something in our defense, ultimately wounding ourselves.

With conscious intention, we can change our minds about anything, mentally retreating for a moment, allowing space from thinking, before taking action, or speaking. In this way, we learn to recognize personal ownership of our every thought and feeling and are less likely to blame someone else for our circumstances, particularly when aligned with a negative thought. Tempering our behaviour enables the space in which we do not immediately have to react from an old belief. There is no longer an urge to suggest to anyone, *you made me do it*. This is a highly empowering scenario, creating responsible behaviour. When we begin to clearly witness our thoughts and feelings in moments of conflict, we can then choose to either react negatively or to proceed positively. It is always a matter of choice, and we can hide our heads in the sand and pretend that we do not own any of our actions, or we can accept ourselves as the creator of our every experience. As we breathe through an uncomfortable condition, it is possible to release and let go, and know that the mould has been broken, or at the least is in a state of shift.

There was a time in my earlier years when I would drown my sorrows by over imbibing in alcohol. It was a cover up and for a time, I was an alcoholic. It began as social interaction with friends, as it generally does with young people, and developed into acutely bad anti-social behavior. My partner and I would often consume two bottles of wine every evening with our meal and then on weekends when partying with friends, the wine would flow in unlimited quantities, quite often rendering me unconscious. The day after I would awake with absolutely no recollection of anything past the meal we had shared, feeling very perplexed that I had *done that to myself again*. The personal cost was heavy indeed as I lost some wonderful friends through that period in my life when I was living unconsciously most of the time. I would now call it the *poor me syndrome* and even though at times I caught a glimpse of the heavy sadness that weighed me down, I had yet to arrive at a personal understanding of how to change the internal beliefs translating into my external world.

It was several years later when I made the definite decision to stop hurting myself and to face my deeper emotional conflicts. I recognized that my heavy drinking was denying me that chance and I knew emphatically that I no longer wanted to blot myself out of reality. Firstly, I acknowledged the painful reality that I was an alcoholic and out of control! I admitted the numerous detrimental effects alcohol had played in my life, not only growing up in company with an alcoholic father, one of my primary role models, but also in overcrowding my mind from being alive and conscious. In such a state of regular obliteration it was easy to dismiss the pain and grief I felt. As I slowly began to awaken, I badly wanted to remedy the denial and rediscover a quality of life. Over time I came to realize the importance of witnessing and identifying issues that disempowered me. In particular, my ability to perceive every person in my life as a mirror for self-recognition, whether for good or bad, became a huge stepping-stone for breaking the shackles. It brought clarity, responsibility, solution and choice about the person I wanted to expose, the authentic soul within. I could no longer blame anybody else for the way I behaved. Those negative aspects that were mimicked from the past could be discarded, creating more spaciousness for meeting myself as I really am. Through dislodgement of emotional pain bodies, my sensitive heart expanded, in turn bringing a heightened sense of truth and an explosion of personal power. Initially it was difficult, due to the resistance from my ego. However, it was the continual whisperings to let go and trust that eventually caught my attention and manifested the changes.

By unlocking the door to your feelings and beliefs, many held tightly in check for decades, and investigating the effects they have played in your life, and may still do, you too can come to understand the power you have to change the aspects you may not like about yourself. It is when you decide to own *all of your baggage* that the doors open and you begin the journey of self-mastery, letting go and healing the wounds of old. No longer needing to cling to the past events that dictated your life, it is an opportunity to modify the way you see the world and awaken to your own creative authority. In understanding that you are capable of being in control of your life's situations through your own free will, provides comprehension for choosing the best possible outcomes and being responsible for all that is within your perceived world. *Seeing* our own behaviour dispassionately, we are able to change what we do not like about it and it is this recognition alone that makes all the difference. Responses to people in your relationships will shift, reflecting your own inner restoration, and bringing an altered state of awareness in the ways you interact with them.

In this world of immense change and transformation, I perceive that it is necessary and a precursor for spiritual enlivenment to squarely face up to what is happening in relationships with partners, family and friends. Any experience of dysfunction on any level, highlights the need for introspection and a check in with ones self to question the cause of such trials and tribulations, and to make conscious intent for shifting that which no longer serves its purpose. In these challenging times, the chaos we are seeing around us and within our own lives appear to be swamping us at an ever faster and furious rate and that is why it is imperative to come into self-understanding. The conditions we perceive in the outer world affect us all on some level of our existence and are provided as lessons for our mental, emotional and spiritual growth. It is time to take stock of what we have personally and collectively created and to take total responsibility for our own actions and the resulting consequences of those actions. If it is harmony, health and well being that we seek, then it is by our own intentions that we will create the necessary changes for manifesting those things into being. Personal responsibility leads to greater accountability for the entire world because we begin to mirror to each person we meet, a preparedness to step into being powerful, receptive and caring, and especially respectful for the good of every other being on the planet. For all the personal work it takes, finding peace of heart is the prize. And what a prize it is.

Message:

> There are no accidents in life, so when you question the validity of the circumstances of your life, then you must expect to receive some negative responses. For if you do not trust yourself completely and the path you chose for yourself, who is it that did that for you? You are the only one responsible, there is no other. Your doubts only serve to create the same old problems in your life and you continue to chase your tail around trying to understand your predicament. You must be still and cease to be so concerned. All is well and it will always be so. This is just a case of trusting self, instead of self-sabotage.
>
> You also have the free will of choosing in each scenario, how to deal with each confronting situation. When you take the responsibility for your own outcomes of either pleasure or pain, this is when the growth for each one of you happens. This eliminates the need to blame and point fingers or to judge another for your own circumstances, whether they are happy or sad, angry or frustrated.
>
> As you walk your path, expect great miracles. Your open, loving trust allows for the flow of abundance to occur. Take care and responsibility for yourself first and then all else will be added unto you. This is your present process, to take care of your own needs first. This will clear the way for you to focus totally on your inspired goals, without hindrance from external concerns.
>
> Your blind faith is what gets you through and your heartfelt knowledge that all is well, at all times. Even when your comfort level drops to zero and you feel the pressure, you know that there is solution in every apparent obstacle. This guides you well and your instincts lead you to take the necessary steps, moment by precious moment. Your vision will clear enabling you to correctly choose the best directives for your goals to be fruitful bearers of your intentions. The ownership for everything is yours.

Do not fear or give any credence to those issues that "appear" to oppose your good. They are only illusory, in that they can create stress and misalignment within you, if you give any power to them. Instead be positive and keep a vision of a happy outcome. By that we mean that you can easily maintain your mental attitude of unification and balance and only "see" the benefits this will create for you. In every situation, no matter how daunting or opposing, lives the means to reconciliation. Already see the issue resolved and then you no longer need to jump into a futuristic mind play, which does in fact, not even exist.

Stay grounded in this resolve and instead of talking and thinking about the negative attributes, only talk and think about what your desired resolution would be. Think only that and talk only that; nothing else.

Do not debate the quality of those people you interplay with. It is all only part of the game and another tool for your growth and development. Stay in the moment and be at ease and peace. Connect only with your heartfelt love and send this out to the people involved. Understand that at a deep level, all incidents, no matter what they appear to be, are designed purely for your sustenance and growth.

You are all one and the same life force energy and therefore your connection with each other also gives the receiver of your outpourings a gift, no matter what form it takes. Be it positive or negative, it is received. Display compassion towards those who you perceive of having faults and values different than yours, for they need to witness your caring attitude in dealings, so they see a piece of them self mirrored through you. These are the acts, which will help to change the consciousness of the world.

This is the most important aspect of personal growth for any soul, as it is intended to ignite a spark of enquiry within each one, to come back to peace and harmony, instead of friction and aggravation. Maintain your ever-loving presence and no matter what, send only love, honour and respect to all that you connect with, in your every day dealings.

From this, you will all come closer together in cooperative liaison and manifest peace and goodwill amongst your selves. This is the reason for the challenges in your lives, so that you can all come into awareness of your brother man and live only from a higher purpose, expressing love and regard for one and all.

As you change your inner perspective of your life and who you are within the game you play, so too will your external circumstances change, in balance, harmony and association with that inner movement. As you expand more and more into the loving being you truly are and express your life from that higher vantage, the things that you no longer need, will fall away like dying bark upon a tree. Let them leave your presence in whatever way naturally occurs, without holding on, struggling or manipulating with your thinking mind. Your higher self will be your accurate guide, so let go and surrender to the moment, knowing that it is all part of the game you play in life.

Inner Guidance:

As issues that challenge your ability to take full responsibility for them arise, step back, create space and take the time to assess your related feelings before reacting. Be prepared to allow emotions to surface, to feel their impact and receive insight into how you are able to resolve the issue at hand. Stay filled with faith during the process, and know you are able to be responsive and self-reliant in any situation.

CHAPTER NINE

You need to wake up

Allow the sleeping giant within you to emerge

DURING MY EARLY TWENTIES, I had an intimate relationship with a co-worker. He was a chef and I a humble server of the magnificent dishes he prepared and presented for consumption to the public. We had not known each other long when *I* decided to move in with him, purely because I wanted desperately to have a loving relationship and thought he would be the ideal partner. On some level, I knew I was just filling in the emotional gaps of loneliness and was no longer prepared to live solely on my own anymore. I had previously shared a unit with a girl friend who had moved to another area, and to have someone in my life seemed better than having no one. I told myself that it would be perfect, that we got along well, had fun together and that he was my best mate. In reality I sold my soul for the opportunity to *supposedly* feel secure. And of course that was the purpose all along, for we were not far into the relationship when I learnt that the man I had chosen as my gap filler, had a wife and two very young children hiding out just around the corner from where we were shacked up. Or was it me who was hiding out?

Daily, on awakening, it seemed as if we were complete strangers. He had his structured routine and I waited in the wings for some interest from him, which never came. We lived separately, as if on different planets and it was not long before I naively realized that things were not going the way

I thought they should. No matter how hard I tried to talk with this man, it was like communicating with a brick wall and I constantly wondered why I had made the choice to connect with him in the first place. Most of our conversations occurred whilst working together and even they were lacking. For a long time I had no idea that he was in fact also having a relationship with his estranged wife, only doors away. Part of me wanted to block out the idea and deny her existence, and so I did and pretended that everything would sort itself out, in the future, some time down the track, when he was over her and wanted to pay more attention to me. What an illusion. I waited and waited, thinking and hoping all would turn out perfectly in the end. My ego was having a field day with me.

Instead of feeling happy and alive, the growing sadness and heart felt pain was overbearing and my self-esteem hit rock bottom. I thought that my contentment depended on being with someone, particularly in a romantic relationship. I felt devastated for a long time, not knowing what to do, only sensing that I was in the wrong place, with the wrong person. Desperately, I decided to take off for a few days in an attempt to gain his attention, and ended up driving hundreds of kilometers across the other side of the country to visit my Dad, hoping somehow it would negate the emptiness I felt welling up inside me. And it did, momentarily; whilst I was there I felt a breath of fresh air and a sense of peace emanate from within the inner turmoil I had been feeling. My mind had a chance to rest and let go of everything. I no longer hooked into feeling inadequate and unloved. It was a breathing space from my constant thinking of ways to make the relationship work, or at the very least, be something it was not.

I then steered my way back home with a sense of renewal and great expectation that I could continue in the partnership and make a go of it. It was up to me, and I drove late into the night to arrive back a day early, eager to see my man again and his reaction to my homecoming. I really thought that things would be different, because I felt different. As I sat waiting for him to finish work in the restaurant, I imagined the elation he would feel because of my return and the resultant affection between us. Instead, when he did finally make an appearance, I was utterly shattered by his indifferent behaviour towards me. His response left me feeling cold and alone, and I had no idea how to deal with the emotions churning within my gut. Feelings of rejection and deflation, self pity and depression began to engulf me and from some distant place within me I could hear the warning bells going off in my head. This was not the way it was meant to be, not in my dreams anyway. How ever was I going to act as if everything was still the same? It was not and never would be. I knew I had changed because I felt peculiar, and understood that my life had taken another turn.

Not long after, feeling somewhat fragile and frightened, but with certainty and clarity I made the decision to leave. I would be entirely on my own and that presented me with great discomfort. To be alone was terrifying and yet in my heart I knew I had no other option. I chose to be courageous; I had *partially awoken* to the fact that this relationship was not going to alter. I was transforming and it felt scary to say the least. If I wanted to break out of the chains that had held me tightly in a very dysfunctional relationship, it was up to me to challenge the voice in my head that spoke of uncertainty, wanting me to play it safe, even at the expense of my personal happiness. I had a glimpse of the old patterns unfolding, particularly after my visit with Dad. It was as if that event had stimulated a lot of the insecurities linking me to men, specifically with achieving a quality, safe union. My father and I had always had our issues, neglect and abuse at times, that had become the blueprint for my continuing relations with men. I now challenged those old systems and deliberately chose to cut the cord of so-called safekeeping in pursuit of my own inner awakening. I realized that it is harder to take the risk and leave a predictable situation, as abusive as it may be, than it is to stay and continue playing the small mind games that bring a morbid sense of belonging nevertheless.

I knew then the significance of those scenarios altering my view of who I am. I had a choice, to stay the same and feel like the doormat, or to leave and empower myself, by taking control of my life direction and becoming self-reliant. I was beginning to attune with my inner self and start to listen to the soft voice whispering in my ear. I heard that I was more than I had thought of myself. I did not need to stay in places, with people that did not serve my best interests. I felt and heard the call to move forward into more of my own influence, creating spaciousness in my life and so I did. The sense of calmness that swept through me, as a consequence of my decision to leave, shocked and amazed me. I felt contentment, perhaps for the very first time. I had decided my own destiny and created the opportunity for freedom and change. By ending the relationship, I began a new one with myself, and it heralded the commencement of more incredible awakenings and even greater prospects for transforming myself.

The messages were there, even then, subtly imploring me to *wake up and let go*, but I did not completely comprehend their meaning then, or the importance of that very special relationship I had shared in. In fact my interpretation was one of letting go of possessions, thinking that to discover more about myself, meant abandoning men and materiality, shedding myself of all, except the bare essentials. It seemed as if *being spiritual* required one to let go of acquisitions, and this I did on every occasion, whenever I moved from one place to another, which was quite frequent. I traveled lightly with only a few treasured items, searching for something or someone to make me feel whole. I was a passionate traveler and I loved the idea of moving on to the next place, for the next experience. On another level however, I was also yearning to meet someone who shared my deep desire for self-realization and understanding, someone I resonated with. As I stepped away from that particular association, feeling free and unhindered, renewed and more alive than ever, ready to spend some quality time alone, was exactly when my spirit offered up another unparalleled challenge. It ushered in even *greater potential* to peel away more of the apprehensive, self-sabotaging layers, bringing with it the guidance to truly stride into my power.

Message:

> *Fear is the illusion of life. It stops you in your tracks and keeps you small and frail. Instead of spreading those glorious wings and heading into the thermals to the heights of creating what you all want you stay on the ground with your tired feet firmly anchored in your self-sabotaging fears. You do yourselves such an injustice. This one thing alone stops your progress and does not allow for the natural flow of trust and love that binds you all.*

> *When you settle into the work you do, you are going to challenge the demons, so to speak, to make a departure from your soul self. The old resident energy from past hurts and traumas is going to surface to be released. It is inevitable as part of the light switch turning on and illuminating all those, no-longer-useful, emotional baddies hiding in the corners of your being.*

> *Be prepared for this from time to time, for the more loving light that flows through your body, the more that disruptions to the old patterns/habits will occur. There is no longer the space for these issues (feelings) to hide out*

in, and so your letting go and trusting will ensure that they surface to be released, through conscious recognition.

In this place, you will be aware that they are only old energy patterns from the past and need to be cleaned up (moved on). Recognize the experience for exactly what it is and in acknowledging the process, you also give permission for the healing that happens within yourself on a deep level. You understand that it no longer has a place in your life now. As you grow and expand in spirit, you can also be grateful for the lesson that surfaced, as a part of your ongoing expansion and empowerment.

Do not get stuck there; it will not serve you to dwell on the issue and try to analyze it. That is the way of the old energy. Recognize, acknowledge and be grateful for the experience it gave you, and the extra space it freed up in your consciousness. Then let it go!

Be free in each moment. Be free. Bear no ills towards those in your life that give you the gift of self-recognition. This is the way that lessons are taught, for each and everyone. It is not personal; it is the gift that you each give to one another, both in the positive and the negative. It is truly beautiful and a blessing you each come with, as human beings on the planet.

Listening in quiet is one of the first steps to take. Listening at all times, will develop within humanity to a stage when there will be no need to find a quiet place to be, but rather to turn ones attention to the power of listening at any time, which will result in acute perceptions in hearing the inner voice of divinity.

Inner Guidance:

Bring awareness into your everyday life by recognizing the daily patterns and onslaught of thoughts that want you to play it safe. With new understanding of how your mind works, you will be able to create the intention for changes that you desire.

CHAPTER TEN

Being is enough

It is in the absence of have to or should, that one finds the stillness and acceptability of simply being

IT WAS DURING THE MOST trying and difficult days, that I came to realize the significance of being, rather than only doing, of acting in some way, generally any way, to make things happen. I learnt the importance of allowing, without needing to pull strings this way and that. I definitely had no other options, for the position I was in made it near impossible to behave any other way than simply *being*. It was a time to be patient and accept the inevitability of life as it is in each moment. The lesson seemed difficult at the time, as they often do. On a deep level I knew it was purposeful, pulling back from reaching out to create another lesson to learn from, thereby compounding the already untenable situation. I found myself uncomfortably out of control and had to sit with it. Many times I thought that I would explode with the intensity of *feeling out of control*, of not knowing, in my head, how to deal with the agonizing, agitated sensations swirling throughout me.

My thoughts would take me to the edge, speaking to me that I should do this, or that I needed to do something else. It took practice for me to still that often-raucous voice that wanted to be in control and take me on a journey of superficial safety. Subtly perceiving the grip of old mind patterns, beyond the emotions, restlessly stirring me up to maintain control, I retreated, uneasily, and observed and learnt and listened as my inner self guided me. Initially it was excruciating as I let go my hold and permitted my higher intelligence to direct the actions. I realized then that I did not have to do anything. I simply needed to be with myself quietly and to still my mind from its constant, overbearing chatter. Eventually, by doing this one simple thing, although it did not at first feel easy, nor comfortable, I felt more in control than ever before.

At the end of each day, Lee and I would relax together and read the message I had channeled. Beautiful, comforting words which resonated with our energy and slowed down the pace of our lives, almost to a standstill. In those moments we knew that we could endure the crisis encompassing us physically. Simply being present moment to moment we were aware that guidance from our higher selves spoke loudly, directing our way and we moved into the reality of *being enough*. Should, or have to, do not play a role when you *feel you are enough*, as you are, exposed and baring your soul. We learnt the important meaning of could, instead of should. As beings of free will, we could choose to do anything, or nothing. There is no rulebook except the one you create for yourself. On the road of learning about whom you are, you discover the power of the mind to take you where it will, often out of control, and you can choose to step back, become alert and learn from simply being silent. You will notice yourself acting out beliefs, many of which do not serve your higher purpose very well. You will see how the mind, your mind wants to take you to places that will keep you safe and comfortable, and often small.

These realizations created an enormous shift in our perceptions and as a result of *being enough within* we outwardly began to manifest positivity into our lives. Books and DVD's such as *The Secret*[6] and *The Passion Test*[7] assisted us to traverse our material world with much more grace and ease. We listened to teleconferences with like-minded positive and motivating teachers and this mirrored our place in time, and my own loving, motivated messages. Our awareness grew and expanded to new levels and our energy soared, even though materially we were still between a rock and a hard place. We felt empowered and *grounded in spirit*, flowing in synchronicity with the events of our lives, whilst attracting everything and everyone to assist us with our preordained plan. We danced every night in celebration, embracing our situation and feeling grateful for the instruction that came with it, offering direction and meaningfulness into our conscious awareness.

We had awakened the sleeping giant within and knew it was time for us to move on. "Being enough" had done that. No more struggling to make something happen, no more needing to work it out and have to, or should. Simply being was enough. Through the process, we did not discount taking action, in accordance with staying present in the moment, and guidance by our higher power. We still lived daily, but differently, no longer relying upon our calculating thoughts to dictate our movements. We listened to our heartfelt thoughts, the spiritual dialogue, and in each scenario decided on the course to take. A highlight of those days was our ability to laugh and sing and not take our lives so seriously. We were able to ride the waves and body surf into shore safely, for we knew without doubt that we were guided every step of the way by a loving divinity inherent within ourselves.

Message:

Being is enough, it is in the absence of have to or should, one finds the stillness and acceptability of the God within. Then there is no more need for striving for one is comfortable in being.

Your feelings may be rife with anxiety around wanting to move either into thinking about the future or the past, which is where the ego mind resides and is most at ease. It is then that being uncomfortable in the process exists and the initial urge is to give in to the mind's desire to return to the old patterns that feel safe. Feel uncomfortable and persist with the process until you begin to realize that you have broken the shackles of conditioning and you feel a new freedom and sense of peace from just being.

Being present in the moment is where life is fulfilling, peaceful, joyful and where miraculous experiences occur. In the ever-present state of being, the source of life energy flows freely through your being and opens you to inspiration, creativity and truth. You reconnect with greater wisdom and inspiring guidance, in every moment. Your awareness expands and you live exceptional lives.

No more battles fought, only one-religion "LOVE", taught in the full scope of being.

No more corruption, manipulation, fear-based decision-making policies. Replaced with love, cooperation, communication and reconciliation, the planet will shine and sparkle in the heavens, radiating an energy that all in the universe will feel at a deep level.

Being as it is, the choices are numerous, the pathways many, and when in doubt for any reason, along the path, the best decision is that of stillness. In not acting when those feelings overwhelm you, the process settles and then allows for the best possible path to open to you. "Being" loving will be the only way, amongst you all on the planet.

Never feel hurried or rushed to complete a task when you do not feel clarity in the action. This is when the mind sweeps you off into directions that do not always serve you best. There is nothing really in life to rush forward into. The passions you feel for your dreams and goals stem from each moment and need readjustments along the way. Be adaptable and know that you set your direction firmly when it resonates from the love you feel in your heart.

Be ever present with yourself. Enjoy the feelings this brings into your life. The simple pleasures of nature's beauty in all its forms; sit with this and discover the true delight in just being. Present in every moment, no matter where you are, or what you do.

This is the true "bible" that you seek. The call of a bird, the rustle of the leaves in the breeze, the warmth of the shining sun, these are the mirrors that lift your soul to ecstatic pleasure and heartfelt truth. This is who I am; existent in all things.

Be patient and enjoy the stillness and quietude; it is a peaceful place to reside and is vital for all healing and manifestation. Through this ability to perceive everything now, we all have the power to create whatever it is we desire. You are creating your reality in each moment and as you celebrate your life in extraordinary ways; your path clears and lightens the way for your vision to unfold in ever growing awareness.

Celebration is joy at being here now. Being happy and light hearted, being constant and optimistic and staying focused on the work you love to do, that of sharing your loving presence with all who are attracted to it. You are able to connect easily with spirit through your faith and knowledge of spirit and this serves you well, no matter what "appears" to be an obstacle in your physical world.

The unfolding of each and every soul is a matter for them, in their own way and time. In the cycle of life, there is no right or wrong, no ups or downs, merely the perception of each being, in alignment with their own journey.

Your life is moving perfectly towards your desired outcomes and passions, and yet it is not the arrival that is important and even necessary, it is the journey, each step you take towards your vision, which serves your purpose. It is the "manner" (manna) in which you step towards your goals, and not the goal itself, which is important.

Blissful living is a state of faithfulness.

Inner Guidance:

Develop patience with others, as this will bring tolerance into your own life and focus you in the present. Impatience indicates when you think you need to hurry because you are running out of time, or that something should have happened already. Let it go and live peacefully within each moment.

CHAPTER ELEVEN

The illusion of separateness

Death is not a possibility, only an assumption of the mind,
in physical manifestation

WHEN I FIRST TOUCHED UPON my brilliant core of shining light, another lifetime ago it seems; I was propelled onto an incredible journey in *search of truth*, mainly ignited by my inherent desire to learn about my genetic relations. I hungered for a functional family, and yearned to bear my own children and develop a sense of *belonging*. Being such a huge event because of my adoptive circumstances, I was eventually rewarded by discovering myself on a much deeper level. Adoption had brought with it some serious boundaries for me to break through, within my emotional self, before I could become a mother. I knew instinctively that I was born to be one, for having asked myself about my purpose, during some heart wrenching moments, I had received the answer very clearly about mothering two children, a boy and a girl. At that time I was single and living on my own, and I could not really "see" how that was going to happen, and yet I just knew it would someday.

I met the father of my children when I least expected to, and in fact I was not interested at all in having a family then. I had just *escaped* from that other very dysfunctional relationship, and I wanted nothing to do with men for a long time to come, particularly if they were married. I had been there and done that more than enough times and I desperately wanted to simply relax and enjoy my own company, free wheeling it for a while. Precisely then is when it happened of course; it was as if the plan of having children had been on the back burner, waiting for the right time and person to enter my life. I fell in love again, with a married man, even though I had no idea he was actually married at the time, and I also knew in my heart that he was the father of my children. Intuitively I recognized him in that role, and although he already had three children from his prior marriage, I felt he was the one, the perfect man, and the father of my children. What made it even more fascinating was the fact that he had also had a vasectomy because he *did not want* any more children. What a spanner that threw in the works! How would I ever conceive the children that I knew were part of our experience together. And if that wasn't enough, I was also grappling with numerous mindsets and insecurities about being a "good mother", the emotional effect of being given away.

I must say, that in those early years when we first met and formed a relationship, I was at my most vulnerable. I tolerated some heart breaking experiences and faced some of my greatest fears squarely in the face. I endured some of the most unpleasant and turbulent times in my life, and with each phase, I grew another inch taller in self-esteem. I chose to go on the rampage, to push past the angry episodes, to get to the heart of my pain and to release old emotions bottled up within me for eons of time. I knew I had to follow the trail no matter what, and I did not give up. Even now when I journey back down my time line, through those memories, etched in my being, I understand the purpose of every event and situation that I experienced. Without those extreme and sometimes brutal manifestations occurring, I would never have opened myself to healing and allowing for the miracles that also ensued. It is definitely true, that existent within every negative situation, is the potential for a greater opposite benefit.

Eventually the vasectomy reversal transpired, an operation resulting in a fifty, fifty chance of success. He had to endure tests and operations and time off from work, and he did this to support my dream. Even though it was not his desire to have any more children, he provided the vehicle for creating them nevertheless, as part of our contract, written before our birth on earth, of which I am certain we came together to fulfill. During this very significant time, we were also delving into alternative healing treatments, such as acupuncture, hypnotherapy and undergoing self-development courses. We were processing a multitude of emotions at a rapid rate and the mental and spiritual changes we made during this period were monumental. As well, we were both searching for our birth mothers, he also being an adopted child with a very strong yearning to establish contact. We were on an amazing journey of self-discovery, mirroring again, the inner desires and intentions we both shared to discern more of who we were, intensely traversing life as one unit.

With emotions running high, came a cross fire of events which plummeted us into a trial separation. We were moving so fast and wanting so much to happen that our stability wavered, sending shock waves through our relationship. In hindsight, we lived totally in each moment, navigating through the doors of chance that began opening, one after another, in all directions. I stayed true to my feelings and lived from my heart, gradually allowing the light to shine a slither of hope into my life. I shuffled from a state of emotional ignorance, to glimpsing my personal power and treading sheepishly through my illusory fears. It was then that I discovered I was pregnant and no words could convey the immense delight I felt. It was an unbelievable synchronistical event, happening just after I had met my birth mother. Having made the connection with her, more than anything else in the world, I had desperately wanted to bear a child. I was ready and had let go the need to control whether it would or would not happen. I had experienced several miscarriages and had surrendered to the bigger plan. I was happy to allow the natural process to run its course. It was a new beginning for us both and our internal shifts in emotional, mental and spiritual growth also ushered in a move of residence and new opportunities reflected outwardly in our physical world.

Throughout my pregnancies, with both my daughter and son, I would dream of them often, physically see them as children and adults and I even knew their names. I attuned to their essence and understood the nature of our spiritual union even before they were born. It was crystal clear to me who they were and the purpose we shared in our journey together. *I remembered we were one*, reconnecting again physically for the purpose of playing once again, another game on earth. The conscious familiarity I shared with them before their births was absolutely pervasive and all knowing. They were my greatest teachers who gave me the special gift of self-recognition by mirroring my own innocent child and I "grew up" with them. In seeking to find myself, my identity, I found much more than I ever expected. I awoke to my spiritual self; my shining being and this enabled me to heal from past childhood pains. I respected their ability to know more and be more than just children. They expressed unconditional love freely, with such unhindered passion, and they radiated wisdom in the simplest forms of being happy in each moment, binding us as one.

In the beginning, they were untouched by the beliefs and conditions that come with time and age. They were innocent, trusting, excited to be exploring life on earth. Growing up, they too learnt the restrictive hand me downs from maneuvering life's highs and lows and the many interactions with people around them. Now the support comes to them as they steadfastly reveal to themselves who they are, once again through their involvement with their children. The cycle repeats and repeats itself, uniting us all in our endeavours to establish our identity with the whole. This is the reality for each and every one of us, and there is no greater purpose in life, than to uncover the truth of who we are, *I am that I am*, connected lovingly with all that is. We have the wherewithal to heal and open up, as loving beings of light, sharing with one and all, as we centre our thoughts on creating a peaceful world to abide in.

Primarily, the quest for knowing one's self is far from the minds of most, particularly because of the conditioned society in which most of us are born. It is however an awakening process that has been sparked off now by the chaos and disorder in the outer world and the many challenges people are being tested with. It is a grand time to understand the roles we play in each other's lives, and to comprehend that the journey is all about recognizing the old innate wounds waiting healing. Not only do we have the ability to know our self through the varied experiences we share with each other, we also have the option to release and heal the energetic pain and fears that have mostly formed our physical existence. From this we discover our individual strength, as well as a loving union with all other beings. It is a meeting of hearts and minds and the connection with one life force. There really is no separation, one from another, therefore we are able to change our view of the world by changing the perception we have of our self, recognizing who we truly are, immortal beings existing everywhere in everything.

Message:

You are never, ever alone. This illusion creates so many journeys of unhappiness for so many souls. Loneliness is a figment of imagination of the mind and does not really exist. In loneliness, people reach out to embark upon courses of action in their lives that do not always benefit them or serve them well. In the process they can become attached to all sorts of harmful substances, including attracting certain people into their lives and methods for creating a negative life style for themselves.

The solution exists in being put and acknowledging the feeling, no matter how bad it feels. Allowing yourself to feel the pain of possible abandonment or isolation gives you some useful steps from whence to rediscover yourself at some deeper level. It is in the depths of despair and darkness that one can find the light-switch to salvation.

This begins the transformation process and the comeback into self identification with spirit and your higher self, connected to the glorious light of loving spirits who surround you and connect with you at all times and in every moment of need.

Do not be disillusioned by the apparent sense of security which you believe dwells outside in your world of physical manifestation. It is not the reality, only the projection of your own mind. The reality is totally the opposite and supports you always in your darkest moments of despair. You are never alone and when you meet up with your true self in cooperation and friendship on your journey, there will be no space, nor need for doubts about your connection with the all loving empowering family of spirit to which you belong.

This is when your life begins to change and you open to a new perspective of your outer experiences in life. No longer will you ever feel alone or give cause to grab at the illusory gap fillers that beckon to you from the external world. You will instead choose to connect to spirit within who guides your journey lovingly, and in this place you will begin to trust and open to the eternal loving source of all of creation, feeling totally safe and never alone.

Stepping through this doorway will lead to the most amazing adventure of self worth and abundance. On your own terms, you will come alive with the gladness to be alive and living a blessed life which is your natural right as a glorious spiritual being.

Left behind will be the doubts, the fears, the neediness of the ego for destructive behaviours and habitual addictions. Not being the foundation of your true self, these perceived attractions would disappear in a flash as you take to securing your identity with the loving spirit that is in fact your real and special self.

Gratification will spring from your inner self-discovery and the knowledge of who you really are. Not from filling up your life from the old mind set patterns and beliefs that do not serve to support your true purpose in life.

You sometimes feel alone and wonder if any other soul feels the same way. You are all one, so you must also be in tune with the same feelings as others. For many, it is a difficult time, as it is a transition in the evolutionary process of the planet.

No one is ever alone and it is only a deception of the outer world, which clouds the inner view and knowledge from those who do not look there (within). It is everyone's birth right by natural process and it is only an unforgotten ability that sets each one on course to feel alone.

It is not the truth, and eventually when all beings recall their divine lineage, it is then that the outer world will appear totally transformed, as will be the human beings themselves.

The truth is, and will always be, that of a loving, divine light energy, pervading the entire universal system, and this can be known and felt within each human experience when the choice is made to search there.

Meditate regularly and breathe in your strength of soul and love from all who support you. Know that you are never alone, and you are dearly loved. Disassociate from separateness and you will have discovered enlightenment. In physical form you appear separate and alone, however this is not the reality. You are connected in spirit and therefore are the enlightened, ever present energy of life.

This work goes way beyond "the idea of spirit", as held by many on earth. This carves through the old misconceptions of spirit (God) being separate and claims the truth of "identification as spirit". In this context, there is nothing other, or outside to fear, or some creepy, crawly ghost, awaiting your selves demise. This is not the truth, only another man made justification to remain aloof and disconnected. The majority are still in this realm of being, in their heads, and will come to realize the truth of who they are and their connection to the whole. Once this "education" reaches their hearts.

Know thyself and all is well.

Inner Guidance:

Our physical world appears to be real and we relate to it individually and separately. Spiritually, it is whole, boundless and timeless. Spirit vibrates throughout existence merging all things. Connect with your soul self and discover the infinite possibilities that abound for you as a divine expression of life.

CHAPTER TWELVE

Taking care of your vehicle

The practice of talking to your cells is one that generates an overall feeling of vitality and wellness

SHORTLY AFTER GIVING BIRTH TO my second child, I recall feeling overweight and flabby. I was very uncomfortable with the unwanted pounds I had acquired and I found it mentally tough to overcome the obstacles contributing to those extra rolls lining my body. Due mainly to the fact that I was suffering emotionally from post-natal depression, I would go on an eating binge and eat several Arnotts cream biscuits each morning and afternoon. It was a craving that became a habit and all too soon instead of thinning down, I was upsizing. My husband began to tell me quite often and emphatically that I was fat, and being extremely sensitive at the time, I began to feel awkwardly self-conscious and unattractive, further accentuating my unbalanced emotions.

In reality, another opportunity was being presented me, so that I could ask myself, "Why am I eating sugary foods?" Why am I being targeted to feel so bad about myself? Why do I need to fill some internal gap in my emotional body by gobbling down comfort food? Why was I so uncomfortable in my skin? Apart from having just had a baby, a major event, I felt there was more to it than that. I had lived in a dysfunctional relationship for a long time, and it was a signal to look once again within myself and "clean out another distressing box that did not serve me well". Even though it irked me terribly to hear the repeated, aggressive comments, it also ignited a switch within me to think about changing what I did not like hearing, and particularly witnessing in the mirror. I *was* uncomfortable and *did* want to alter the pattern of behaviour I was living, and I was really grateful that I was being reminded unwittingly to alter the course I was on.

One morning after another hurtful attack, I reacted angrily and *made the decision* to alter what I did not like hearing about myself. I knew it was only up to me, for I had realized long before that the power to create changes comes from within oneself. Firstly, as hard as the thought was, I decided to stop eating so many sweet biscuits. I loved those scrumptious, sugary treats and looked forward to the pleasure they gave me. I also knew they had become a habit much like any other addicted substance and were not a healthy choice for my body. I planned to replace them instead with a nutritious snack, or some fruit. I knew it was more about mind over matter than anything else, and I was determined to stick to my newly formed plan. *The idea itself enlivened me greatly.*

Next stop, the health and fitness centre in our local area, where I began the grueling process of regular exercise. Previously, when embarking upon a work out program, aerobics had been my pick of the bunch, rather than jogging or running. I love the set routine and being guided through the steps, along with the funky music. To me it was like dancing which is fun, fun, and more fun, and also very freeing. So off I plodded to partake three times a week and found it excruciatingly hard work to begin with. I would return home absolutely spent, almost unable to stand up. But I was sick to death of being put down, and in fact the words being hurled at me were merely mirroring my own self-dissatisfaction. The anger and frustration I had initially felt gradually dissolved, bringing a transformation of my self-esteem. I built up strength and flexibility in my body, releasing the old emotional patterns with every step I took. Within a couple of months of disciplined effort, both with the dietary and exercise routine, those extra flabby rolls vanished, and I not only looked far healthier but felt absolutely terrific.

As the months passed I began to feel "my powerful self" again, the beautiful person I am, and I realized that taking care of my body was of primary importance physically, mentally, emotionally and spiritually. My radiance and confidence returned and the quandary that I had previously felt began to melt into oblivion. I no longer received the hurtful insults and that was a huge plus. Even though the workouts were grueling initially, my *decision* to take the first step, the action to change what I didn't like about myself, were well worth the gains and the effort it took. I learnt the value of listening to the external messages that came to me from the people within my sphere of being. Instead of begrudging the comments that had slapped me across the face, and feeling small and pissed off, I chose to be responsible, taking action for changing what I really wanted for myself on a deeper level. I understood the significance of growing with the occurring events and owning the power to revolutionize them. I know how each of us is able to modify the things we do not like. My first step was acknowledgment of the creator within me.

With awareness of the holistic approach, and being receptive to my body's functionality, particularly when I feel the launch of pain or sickness is of great benefit. I ask my higher self for direction and guidance, intuiting the appropriate emotional cause for the dis-ease. In this way, I converse with the cellular structure of all the bodies, enabling healing and easing of the physical symptom. This can occur through breathing, visualization, stretching or exercise. Generally, when I am feeling physically sick, I know the reason is due to an energy block and I communicate with the cells in the area of my body that requires the healing. Sometimes, I will intuit a need for resting, a change in diet, or drinking more water for cleansing. Quiet time in meditation, breathing, clearing the chakras and freeing the energy flow can also be constructive, as may a walk in nature, a climb up a mountain, or a stroll along the beach. Other times, shouting out in anger, or crying has helped, thereby releasing pressure held in a particular area of the body, releasing emotional pain whilst recalling the effect of prior life trauma. Also being guided to another healer, such as a naturopath, herbalist or counselor.

Generally, in our society we have learnt to lean heavily on the outside world for everything we need in our life. When we get a cold or the flu for instance, we head straight to the doctor for antibiotics or to the chemist for some sort of pill to fix us up. We have become dependent on the health system to make us feel better and to tell us what to do, by administering drugs to alleviate our physical pains. I remember my doctor from many years ago telling me once, that most of his patients only came to see him to talk about the many troubles confronting them in their daily lives. All they were really seeking was a confidant to share with, and he became that friendly listener. Quite often the person would leave with a reassurance that they were perfectly healthy without needing any other thing. His role was to act as a sounding board, counseling them gently to understand their own emotional dis-ease. Certainly there is no inference that doctors do not hold relevance in our society, for there are many specialist services required. However, somehow down the ages, perhaps without conscious intent, we have forgotten or misplaced our innate ability for self-healing. As individuals we all own the power to heal our bodies, on all levels of being.

Learning to listen to our physical body, in fact *all of our energetic bodies* is an important factor and hugely enjoyable in the healing process. If we can turn our view inwards and become reliant on the messages we intuitively hear, we are a very long way along the path of self-healing. We are *all* capable of maintaining excellent health by staying focused and alert to our body's communications by way of aches and pains. When we ask the question, "What is it I need to know about this situation?" the answer we seek will always be provided, either through intuition, symbology or a synchronistic event occurring. By shifting our perception of who we are, and trusting ourselves implicitly, we begin the process of conscious connection to the source of our creativity. We will always be guided to a solution, even if it is not what we essentially think it should be. Often we will be challenged to confront some imaginary fear, and to penetrate the mental obstacle obscuring our deeper insights.

Taking care of our vehicle, the one we were born into is of utmost importance if we are to live a fulfilled and worthwhile life on earth. We came for the purpose of staying alive physically for as long as we planned, different for each and everyone of us, and particularly learning from the unique set of circumstances applicable to each of us. The idea is to enjoy the vitality of a healthy body and to respond to the changes in our lives with mental dexterity and positivity. Even when we are faced with the challenges of daily living and the bigger world around us, we are able to maintain our bodies in prime condition. If we allow the stem of external negative illusions to take over, through bombarding our minds with media hype and manipulation, and a dependency on drugs and pills through advertising, then we are prone to lose our way and become reliant on others for our health, and thus our perspective of life. If we go along with every word and picture we hear and see on our television sets, we are handing over our power to others. In a sense we are being brainwashed into believing what other people think, instead of having faith in our own personal instincts and judgments.

As is the nature of life, we can either choose to free ourselves from old conditioned restrictions, and be healthy and happy, finding contentment in living a long time, or we can stay stuck in the perceived comfort zone of old habits and crutches we have learnt to rely on most of our lives. To change and grow is to get uncomfortable from time to time and we must step beyond our fears, let go our hold, and unite as one with our divine essence to guide our way. This is not to say our life becomes a flat line of constant health, which is the ultimate potential, however it does imply that we alone take charge of determining the outcome we desire to achieve, by eating healthy foods, exercising regularly and taking necessary time out to play and relax, stimulating our senses in positive ways. I find it is also constructive to mentally hold an impression of a healthy, strong physical body, capable of renewing the cells within it regularly thereby creating longevity. As we continue to progress, we are learning to become familiar with the cellular structure of our bodies. At this particular time on the planet, Scientists are delving deeply into areas specific to our DNA and observing some remarkable attributes yet to be adequately explained, mainly because aspects of the data are still beyond scientific comprehension. Multidimensional in nature, and perhaps beyond our current scope to logically appreciate, our energetic spiritual self holds the information channel that directs the machinery of our physical bodies. I am sure that over time, there will be innovative discoveries ushering in a higher perception of the infinite possibilities that already await us to transform illness and disease into optimum health.

Message:

> *Your body is your most precious vehicle of expression and when it feels uncomfortable on some level, it then indicates a shift occurring for your conscious awareness and release. On some level, emotions have settled and if not addressed can create a build up of long-term disease within the cells. To avoid this happening, it is vital to clear yourself regularly of the distressing energy build up, and to practice this through both inner and outer bodywork.*

Releasing the built up emotional energy that does not sustain your spirit is the process of healing your "inner bodies" as well as nourishing the physical body. As pain surfaces in the body you begin to recognize it as the effects of past emotional conditioning causing physical and emotional distress and this can be easily released.

The practice of talking to your cells is one that generates an overall feeling of vitality and wellness. In this simple procedure, one can restore the cells to their optimum energy level and this will maintain the body's overall health.

Communication at the cellular level is achieved by understanding that the physical body is an energy machine, alive and receptive to information transference through your intention and positive thoughts. It is through the intention to release negative energy and to breathe regenerative loving light energy into the cells that this is achieved.

When you feel the tightness in your body and the urge of the ego (mind) to grip and hold onto these old patterns, you can then allow the pains to surface in the body and recognize they are only the effects of past emotional conditioning causing distress and can be easily released. Relax your body with meditation practice, as this is the greatest gift you can give to your body, supporting it to live freely (of any stress). Exercise and fitness are essential tools for the body's maintenance and wellbeing.

Being well is a choice, of living from heart or head. The choice is in understanding the difference and being able to decide that you are free in every moment, to be a loving light in human form, instead of a human living from a conditioned mind. The body follows the conscious state. Fertilize the mind with divine energy of abundance and the body will follow suit. Still the mind of its erratic behaviour and divine guidance will flow through to channel wisdom.

You are energetic atoms of life. The form (the human body) is replicated from millions of cellular possibilities, creating individual forms that are born, a manifestation of conscious intention in spirit. In manifestation anything is possible, whatever the consciousness intends to create. The power of manifestation is an aspect of spirit; and it is intention that is the catalyst for creation; intention to be; whatever comes from conscious thought.

A new energy emerges which is full of love, co-operation and balance with the old paradigms which you grew up with. This shift is shaping many new experiences in peoples' lives and is most apparent in the health arena. Many "older" people are stepping into their own energy source for healing and creating an extended life on earth.

There are really no barriers to the age a human can live, except that which the mind will dictate. Fitness and health are paramount in this newly emerging energy field and it will continue to progress on many levels, uncovering new ways to support the human life system whilst on earth.

As minds expand to encompass these changes, so will the human body co-operate with itself (higher) in bringing about a substantial decrease in physical and mental health. So much of the human health issues relate to the stressful lifestyles lived by so many and this will decrease when the alignment of spirit and body takes place internally. Reliance on "self" for healing will be the new paradigm, rather than an external crutch that is (now) currently of the old system.

It is in the deeper recesses of the being where the real healing takes place, which is permanent. So much of humanity relies on an external diagnosis for betterment, when it really only takes an energy transference to heal oneself at the core. The process is simple and yet profound. No matter what you "feel" like in your body, your spirit soars in delight and wonder at the magnificence of life. "You" in human form are subject to the emotional roller coaster ride of your everyday lives, and this is why the practice of "being still," returns you to the indwelling of peace and rest.

In your wisdom and knowledge of spirit, when you follow your innate guidance system, no amount of turmoil in your physical world will disrupt your balance for long. You will know to return home to the inner spiritual connection that provides you the strength and courage to move through any experience with faith in its purpose. Trust that your guidance system carries you in the best possible way and that as long as you do not bend to the ego's urgings to give in, you can live a life as big as you can ever imagine.

Inner Guidance:

Come to rely on your self for your own health's sake. Trust the guidance you receive from your body as it always lets you know when a blockage needs releasing. Speak the language of love to your body reinforcing the message through intention to be healthy and well.

CHAPTER THIRTEEN

Balancing your life

Dance with yourself and ease the tension

DANCING FOR ME IS A beautiful reminder of my early childhood days. I grew up in a family of great upheaval, where both my parents worked and arriving home late and tired they would regularly argue over some trifling thing or other. My father was generally liquefied from having had quite a few beers at the pub and this would be the impetus for the ensuing onslaught of angry words fired off between them. Often, after sitting anxiously through the nighttime meal, I would eagerly disappear outside wanting desperately to escape from the acute tension pervading the house. I would twirl and spin and dance around the spacious backyard in absolute abandon, letting go the burden of propping up the heavy, distressful feelings churning within me. When I was totally spent and out of breath, I'd flop down onto the lush green lawn, silently gazing up at the radiant magnitude of stars, feeling utterly at home, and for a moment, at peace with myself once again.

It wasn't until much later in my life that I realized the powerful, healing effect dancing regularly gave me. The activity alone was like taking the lid off a pressure cooker and releasing the hot steam into the ethers, thus allowing my body and mind to unleash the constant tension surrounding me. Innocently and without conscious thought, I had obeyed my instinct to move away from the negative energy brought on by my parents' continual squabbling, and found an essence of harmony and balance provided with the positive motion of dancing, which I loved. Always completed with a silent meditation amongst the glorious stars, ensuring a calmness and blissful state of being. In its way, dancing gave me a lifeline to sanity and reminded me of whom I was, instead of where I was. Linking with the galaxy of stars brought me back home, in my heart to a place that felt very familiar and comforting. Balancing the negative with the positive, providing me with a safe haven in which I could live, not always happily, but at least from another optimistic perspective.

In those quiet moments lying on the healing green grass, enfolding me like a soft blanket and bringing comfort, it was as though the world stood still and I had no concerns, no complaints and I just was. I existed in a perfect state of stillness and all the quarrelsome noise and frantic anxiety expressed around me had no substance. I was alone, on my own and yet I felt as if I encapsulated all things. I loved those moments in my childhood and they supported me as I grew and traversed the regular daily involvement with my family. I knew I could rearrange my space to create harmony and balance if I chose to, or needed to. Stabilizing the impact of such negative surrounds was vital to my wellbeing and I was very thankful for growing up with those peculiar conditions so that I could understand my capacity to deal with them in such a vital way.

Even now, one of the greatest things I share with my two beautiful grandsons, and now my granddaughter is dancing. As I did with my own kids growing up, we have some wonderful, fun filled times where we rock around the lounge room, singing and laughing wholeheartedly. Jayden the oldest, learnt the simple "art of dancing" as a baby, when I would twirl him through the air as I moved to the fantastic beat of "The Lion King". As he grew older, whenever music was being played, his young body would begin to gyrate as if on auto pilot and his little feet would move from side to side in perfect rhythm with the vibe of the song. He would still be dancing well after I had collapsed happily in a heap, exhausted and out of breath. What exhilaration we would feel, along with a great sense of fun and wellbeing, and a gladness to be alive. It certainly aided with getting them off to sleep, which they did soundly for the entire night.

In some ways, I feel that since the inception of technology, with children's movies, computer games, game consoles and mobile phones, all being readily available to kids from a very early age, the simple acts of play and dance have been substituted. The relevance of exercising the body and mind with activities that promote health appear to have been replaced with the mesmerizing, almost addictive behaviour of eyeballing a computer screen or ipod. Gratification is no longer sought from within, but from gadgets that every child, to feel good, has to have. Consumerism is alive and well, however, are our children as able-bodied. Today's technology is a wonderful, worldwide connection we can all share, certainly bringing us into closer proximity with the one world at large. It is an extension of who we are and what we are capable of creating. Sometimes however the basics of *simply being* are overlooked. The media onslaught of information, be it negative or positive, can invade our personal world and if we are not conscious of its effects, it can become a replacement for not having to think for ourselves.

In the perceived busy world of having to have, is life balanced and are our bodies maintaining a healthy vitality? Complementing materialism with spirit is the call. We can have it all, health, wealth and happiness in true equilibrium when we connect from within first and foremost. Satisfaction in our home life, with family and friends is paramount. If we take away the material gadgets from our existence, what we have left are the people we interact with. This is a priority for me, bringing a harmonious and abundant life. If our children are playing on their machines day in and day out, are they available to see, hear and feel the reality of the world within them. Or are they turning off because of what they would rather not see and hear. In a seeming troubled environment, where life appears to be an ongoing struggle, due mainly to our learnt programming, are we providing the best opportunities and outcomes for one and all to discover and expand as spiritual beings?

Understanding the need we all have to live harmoniously and happily, respecting each other. This is balance. "Things" do not necessarily do it for us. They can be the distraction from what is important, such as relating with each other. When I hear people say that they are bored, I wonder what they are bored with. Perhaps it is their inability to enjoy life without having to do something, or to watch or play with some doodad. Learning to sit with ones self silently has not been paramount in our western world teaching. Make time to play with each other. Dance with one another. Grow with one another. Learn with each other. Be outside with nature and smell the roses, dance to the moon, delight in the simplicity of being and balance material life with the natural pleasures that abound in totality around us and within us. It is again up to each and every one, to create the changes we desire in our lives, through our intention. Intend to live a balanced and happy life. Have frequent conversations with your self, your higher self. Push the activate button on your set, the one that resides within you.

Message:

You all hear the inner call to freedom. This is freedom from the self-imposed restrictions to your soul. It is the man made regulations and requirements to live your lives from the outside in, rather than from the inside out. When you feel the pressures of the outside world crowding in on you, this is the time to stop and impose a "regulatory approach" to the situation. It is when you need to sit quietly and reflect on the reality of your life experiences. It is time to free your self from the shackles of material obligation and pursuit.

Remember your humanness and do not expect so much from yourself as you do. You need to take care of your bodily needs first and foremost, so get plenty of rest, exercise and take plenty of time out for fun and play.

Relax your self, for you do not have to "do" anything. The world spins round in a constant spin and it always will. You can take your time to enjoy each moment and live it fully alive in the present time. There is never a rush to go here, there, or anywhere, except that created in the mind with your thoughts of "have to" or "must do". Doing is man made, and even though in each moment you are doing, even relaxing is a doing thing.

The more relaxed you stay, the less stress in your body and mind, and the more power you generate. You are actually refreshing your self and enabling it to "do" more things, in fact. The practice of relaxing regularly in your life creates a balance and is necessary for your overall wellbeing. You will achieve more from this state of being than from feeling that you should be up, off and keeping busy.

When you "do" work, play, whatever it may be from this relaxed state, you are "enjoying" the activity you are involved in, and this satisfies the soul and creates a sense of joy and satisfaction, rather than a stressful, resistance to the task.

The more you do from a relaxed state, the more you can do. By centering yourself daily and breathing into your body and releasing the urges to "do", you can increase your energy and your consequent ability to achieve so much more. The process also allows for the natural flow of life energy to create more of what you want in your life, rather than an obligated sense of "have to".

You may well encounter some mental resistance to relaxing when you first start, because the old habit must be broken. You're chattering mind will attempt to dissuade you in any way it can, and one specific way is through a sense of "guilt"; either for letting someone down, being lazy, or some other reason. The voice of ego will try anything to sabotage your new intention, so be aware and alert to these feelings within yourself and counter the voice in your head with a positive affirmation, that relaxation is serving your highest good.

Learn to develop your ability to "notice" the mind games taking place in your thoughts so that you can immediately shift back into the present time and stay relaxed. Any negative feeling such as guilt, come from past conditioning and do not necessarily serve your life now. Living a fulfilled life comes from "being present" and maintaining a high level of energy. Be fully aware in every moment, of your surrounds and stay focused on your desires and goals.

Be at peace with yourself in all things and choose to do only those things that you love to do. Embrace the challenges when they come and step your way through them. Maintain your focus, relax and breathe, releasing the stress.

Bridge the gap between your outer world and inner world and transform your lives. Find a balance in your external structures with your internal habitat. Reverse your priorities and live firstly from the connection with spirit to create all the abundance you could ever wish for in the material world.

Planet Earth represents your own revolutionary process. As it turns full circle on its own axis, so do you human beings. Your axis is your centre and therefore it maintains your balance and control in your physical body. If you go off balance from your axis, your body suffers due to an irregular alignment, and being off-center.

Rest in the quietness of your being, at anytime in any place; this brings balance and harmony to an otherwise apparent, chaotic world. Move into your soul body by being "internally active", as well as externally. In this way you can balance your self and feel inner peace.

Anchor your self in spirit and live a life of love, passion, enlightenment, joy, fun and laughter, as the daily unfolding manifests abundantly.

Stillness awakens the beast; and in this quiet state of being, the "power of one" emerges, leading one in each moment to be everything and create anything.

Guidance comes with every step of the way, in every "being moment". Harness the power within each cell of your being and direct it towards your heart felt desires.

Inner Guidance:

Focus your attention on your spiritual self more often. Turn the television set off and pay less attention to the media commentary. Be less distracted by computer games, or any other technical gadget and enjoy the beauty of outdoors. Choose to spend regular time with yourself in quiet reverie.

CHAPTER FOURTEEN

I came with a purpose

Being in action with your soul's purpose is the key to happy and joyful living

EVER SINCE I CAN REMEMBER, I have felt an immense innate sense of helping people, some how? By the time I was in my mid teens, I desperately wanted to speak seriously with my father about why he had treated me the way he had. It was not to get angry with him, or judge him; rather it was my own self-analysis that was important. I wanted to determine the how and why of my conditioning, so I concluded that going directly to the person of greatest influence in my life, would be the best assistance. An opportunity came one evening after dinner, when I gathered the courage to go to his room and ask if I could talk to him. Amazingly his attention was fully focused on me and when I questioned him, he answered many of my queries with an emotional capacity I had never seen or heard from him before. His replies genuinely surprised me with their honesty, and I instinctively knew he stored great sadness in his heart. My initial anxiety was replaced with a sense of compassion for the life he had led, and we silently hugged for many minutes, an expression of unconditional love that I cannot recall sharing since sitting on his lap as a young child. That sublime moment was the stimulant for a seed of awareness that surfaced, albeit a tiny fraction, of a natural ability I stored in my own heart.

Along my path of learning, I found that a lot of my life experiences led me to delve into the depths of my being, looking for answers about my circumstances and situations, and this I did continually. I wanted to know more than appeared on the surface of my daily life. I wanted to understand what I was doing here, in this physical expression. I wanted to create a quality life, something that seemed to elude me, certainly in my younger years. I felt that something was missing from my world and yet I saw other people around me who appeared to be achieving their dreams and goals. Still, I could not figure out how to make my vision a physical reality, and I really yearned to understand what my life purpose was. I had spent many years in self-contemplation and was ready to have a light turn on and reveal a pathway that would adhere with my intuitive sense of being of service.

My answer came several years ago, when an opportunity arose for me to embark upon a wonderful "Mystery Tour"[8] to Colorado, with eleven other participants. The course was a five-day event and each participant had to congregate at a certain time, on a certain date, at a prearranged location. And then do what, I had no idea? The journey to get there was in itself an adventure and I felt very excited about travelling to the United States and seeing places I had never been before. Let alone partake in an unknown schedule of mysterious excursions to who knew where. At the same time, I was very unsure of where my life was heading and a part of me was expecting some answers to some serious questions I had been asking myself for quite some time.

As the event drew nearer, my anticipation of the expedition heightened and I sensed that unfamiliar knowledge would open me to new possibilities and ideas, of which I had no insights at the time. As I was browsing in a bookstore about a week before leaving, I had one of those magical moments where the book you *need* stares out at you from amongst the pile of others of which it is assembled. As the energy of the book's contents beckoned to me I reached out and flicked through the pages. The one that opened to me was the preface and the words that grabbed my attention stood out like giants on the page. I could not miss their message, miraculously reflecting my internal dialogue at the time. Part of the passage read, "we know nothing" and the profundity of those few words mirrored precisely how I had been thinking for several days leading up to the trip.

I was in a state of limbo not knowing what direction to take. My head felt like a hazy cloud, with no apparent ability to comprehend any of the calamities occurring in my life. I suddenly realized that I had that same feeling of knowing nothing, as the book had implied, and it somehow allied me to a sense of freedom. I no longer needed to think of anything, I no longer needed to understand how to fix every little thing. In fact, I had absolutely no idea how to anyway; certain circumstances in my life were so out of my control. The profound impact of those few golden words, gave me a glimmer of insight that I took with me on the journey, energized by the prospect of what lay before me. Interestingly, as a group on our first day, we were asked what it was we predominantly wanted to gain and understand about ourselves along the way. I simply stated that "I knew nothing" and that it was my intention to explore the meaning of that perspective.

It came as no surprise that as we journeyed amongst some of the most beautiful, majestic and inspiring places on the planet, I began to comprehend the significance of *knowing nothing*. How can one possibly, from a human viewpoint with a finite mind, understand the creation of soaring mountains and how the natural world exists? I took the book[9] with me, along for the ride of a lifetime, and it gave me far more pleasure and enlightenment than I can possibly express in words. The sheer beauty of nature that supported my passage enabled me to discover the same inner beauty that I am myself, connecting me with the spirit of life on a deeply inspiring level. I let go my logical mind and attuned with, *not knowing*, and discovered much more than I ever thought probable. The grandeur and the simplicity, the all-pervasive presence of divinity and wisdom was highlighted everywhere. I communicated with the trees, I could identify their faces energized in the trunks, and the majestic mountains and valleys covered in deep snow spoke to me of life immemorial, mirroring my own spiritual nature. I stood on top of the world, gazing out at the limitless panorama, unafraid and knowing nothing. I glimpsed the native people who had built amazing stone homes and sacred sites in inexplicable places eons before and felt the deep underlying essence within myself in everything.

In the final days of that amazing adventure into the depths of my soul, I had the most honoured occasion to meet, as we all did, a most remarkable person of Native American origin. It was the icing on the cake and the experience is one that lives in my heart eternally. In his wisdom, he pointed the way for me to *step up* into my higher being. In his unique communiqué, he questioned me to confront the small game I was playing in my life, challenging me to come out of my well guarded cave and take a bigger peek at who I really am. I knew irrevocably, that I received the answer to my question, "what is my purpose?" and that it was up to me, to step up to the line and take action by living it. I knew in my heart that I was here on earth to shine a light for other people to know themselves, as I myself had done.

I arrived home knowing that I wanted to embark upon the path of my particular purpose and I asked myself many questions and listened for the answers. I had realized on the trip, that to acknowledge that I knew nothing was also to accept that I knew everything. A hard one for the ego to comprehend, as it wants to trip us up and keep us thinking small, the game I had until then been playing very well. I no longer wanted to wear the mask of fearing success by not taking action, which had held me back for a lifetime. I wanted to break through all of the barriers that blocked my way to living on purpose, and it was my intention then and there to reach to the depths of my divinity and begin expressing myself through my highest power.

Meeting me head-on were the everyday issues and financial dilemmas that had been temporarily put on hold. Yes they still existed in a time and place that I was required to deal with, however my heightened perceptions had brought a shift in the way I viewed them. I could envision a much more positive outcome, dealing with the challenges more easily by not worrying so much. More than anything, I wanted to step into my powerful self and live from my heart centre instead of only my head, which I also realized had not always been the best choice. My intention to stand taller, energetically, was the impetus that opened my heart chakra, thus enabling a clearer vision and mental pathway for creating more of who I am.

I knew without any doubt, that I was far greater than I had thought myself to be, and that I could do anything that I set my heart on through intention and commitment to the task. Clearly, my life purpose was to enhance people spiritually, as I had done for myself by unlocking my own door of wakefulness to recall my *true* self. I was now walking hand in hand with my higher source and I trusted the guidance I would receive moment to moment. I recognized that we all come into physical being "owning" a life purpose. Whether we remember or not is for each and every one of us to explore, if we choose. I received messages on the mystery tour from many wise souls, and I chose to follow the path of discovering my own soul's purpose. It has led me to greater understanding of my capabilities and unique command to express that principle through living it.

Interestingly, the 'Colorado Mystery Tour' was presented by Brendan Nichols, author of the book "Your Soul Purpose". About a year before going on the mystery tour, I had been reading the local paper and came across an article about Brendan and his newly published book. I was immediately attracted to the title, simply because I had been consciously asking for direction about my own purpose. I jumped onto his website and purchased the book and consequently attended several more of his seminars. In the ensuing period I attained some personal breakthroughs that enabled me to consciously comprehend the relevance of my initial question.

I also discovered that aligning with my soul's purpose manifested everything I needed to accomplish that function. I experienced events at times that were both challenging and rewarding and the emotional ups and downs brought tears of elation and sadness as I boldly traversed the path towards my vision. I saw that I needed to release the old ego patterns of fear and scarcity thinking along the way to allow my being to grow in expanding awareness, connecting with and healing my emotional and mental bodies. The messages I received were the foundation for both my recovery and my inspiration. They buoyed my confidence and faith and gave me hope. If I was the only one who ever read them, then I had fulfilled a desire of lifting myself out of the abyss I had felt trapped in. The healing effect the beautiful words had for me was profound. Quite simply, I was shown that when I focused my full attention on being present, my life flowed in synchronicity, versus mentally controlling a situation with logic alone. By giving space to a problem, being uncomfortable for a time and breathing through it, created another reference point from which to work. I was making a conscious choice to let go of the need to dictate the outcome.

My purpose simply became one of spiritual connection and expressing myself through writing the messages. As the words streamed onto the pages, I felt more and more at home, and far removed from the negative aspects and events occurring simultaneously. Even during the chaos, the light shone brightly in my life and I learnt the significance of gratitude for every momentary event, be it testing or rewarding. My spirit soared and my mental clarity motivated me to take the necessary action to commence the task at hand, knowing that inner guidance was always my companion. As it was then, and still is now, the greatest pleasure comes from the support of my spiritual family, always there, always available.

Message:

Find your purpose and take action to achieve that purpose.

Get out of your comfort zone human being and commence the journey that is the only real, true and proper course for such wondrous beings. Live the life you were born into and know that you are the essence of life itself.

When this is done, simply, you shall feel more comfort, pleasure and peace than at any other time in your lives. Have faith in the process of life, it is no accident that you are here in this very state of existence, except to change the status of your soul; to be truly alive and light up the world with your very presence.

When you realize your connection with all (the living spirit), you have no need to fear. You step up to the line and the most amazing opportunities present themselves, not always as your conditioned mind thought of. When you have total trust in this process, then miracles occur. This is the blessing of the divine source, who resides within you at all times. What peace this brings.

In reality, one can never really deny their true calling, no matter what they choose to embark upon. Spiritually it is the only way, for after all, that is your true identity and the tasks you chose to perform on earth were all decided upon, in your spirit state before your birth.

Your energy resonates with your purpose and once you come to surrender to its calling, your life then takes on new meaning. Your health, wealth and happiness improve because you now resonate with the truth of your journey on earth; that which is aligned to your true purpose for being on earth.

Like a magnet, you attract all the necessary pieces and parts into your life for fulfilling your purpose. Your renewed sense of direction creates clarity and you feel free to embark upon your life's journey with faith and confidence, knowing that the fit is in perfect synchronicity with your higher self's intention.

Consciously, you will come to understand that you alone have the power to change your life's experience. No longer content to "put up with" a life unfulfilled, you will step through fears and boundaries that you set for yourselves in the old energy and recreate a life of purpose.

The desire and curiosity for something more fulfilling in life will be the catalyst, and spark the enquiring mind into action. Instead of settling for the everyday routine and toiling in work and positions that do not fit the soul's purpose, action will be taken in pursuit of joyful, giving expression of one's true passionate abilities.

Simply step into your purpose and begin now to live the life you came to live. That is all. Jump each hurdle in the moment as it appears, confidently going forward to create your dreams and knowing who you are.

Surrendering to your mission and aligning with your higher self in accomplishing the goals you came to earth to achieve and living true to your hearts desires you are now embarking upon your chosen path.

The evolvement of the human race means an expansion of each individual in harmony with each one's life purpose, and the uncovering, so to speak, of one's purpose in living and being a part of this evolutionary process taking place now on the planet.

It is a great time to rejoice. Many, many, many hearts are opening and hearing the true calling of expanding and living a life from purpose, rather from the old paradigms and mind sets of past beliefs. Great moves of energy and shifts in consciousness are the outcomes; when millions and millions and millions usher in the new wave of realization of oneness within themselves.

The flow of energy, based on enthusiasm and total commitment for one's true purpose will ignite the impetus of the creativity juices and expansion of spirit will result. The lessons along the way are what propels and encapsulates the purpose.

Step by step awakening and trusting in the connection we each have with the divine source will enable us to overcome any obstacles and challenges. Fully committed and energized, one will walk hand in hand with one's higher self in harmony and co-operation in achieving the purpose of being here and now.

Be still in the full knowledge that there comes a time in everyone's life for trans-formation. There are no accidents or coincidences. You all come (into earth) bringing within your essence the key components necessary for your *lives' unfolding. You move from rung to rung in synchronicity with your life direction.*

No one is different from any one else. We are all the same. The only difference for those that have become successful is that they didn't give up, stop, or turn back when the going got tough. They resolved to keep on purpose with their dreams and passions. Nothing stopped them. Having purpose ignites the internal engine and drives you forward along your path, so continue with your vision and determination to achieve your purpose.

Inner Guidance:

Knowing and understanding your purpose gives direction to your life. If you do not already have a sense of that, ask your self for guidance and be open to hearing the answer. Purpose provides fulfillment and joy and offers an abundance of opportunity to be of service, opening your heart to happiness for one and all.

CHAPTER FIFTEEN

Greatness is your birthright

Greatness comes from perseverance

DURING THE COURSE OF ATTENDING numerous seminars to learn from the gurus of real estate and self-development, particularly highly successful people such as Robert Kyosaki and Dolf DeRoos, perhaps the single most important part I learnt about achieving success and prosperity was that of *perseverance*. Not only was that trait a by product of those people's success, it was continually stated and restated repetitiously so that one could get it planted firmly into one's psyche. Some of the stories of accomplishment in fact came from those individuals who continued time after time, no matter what the challenge, or the delay or decoy, to maintain focus until they had achieved their goal. Even after continual failure, it seemed that passion and heart, combined with perseverance, were the necessary ingredients in accomplishing the desired end result, no matter what the target.

Once you have mentally affirmed your goal and crystallized it within your heart, it is essential to maintain vigilance as you walk towards achieving that objective. When I was in my early twenties, a couple of friends at the time decided to travel overseas and a group of us went to farewell them at the airport. I felt extremely excited on the day, not only for our companions heading off on the trip of a lifetime, but also at the prospect of journeying to some far off foreign destination myself. My passion for travelling was embedded in my being and I would often visit the airport on weekends just to watch the planes take off, dreaming of being on a magical mystery tour to some exotic location around the world. As we waved our friends off on their extended journey, the rest of us, being four couples, sat and exuberantly planned an overseas trip of our own. Then and there, we all committed to boarding a plane within twelve months, igniting our own overseas adventure, exactly as our friends were doing.

Weekend after weekend, we would all congregate and talk incessantly of nothing else, adding support to each ones desire to achieve the dream. We set a departure date for the same time the following year, and my partner and I also planned how much money we would need to save for return flights, sightseeing, as well as living expenses for a few months if work was unavailable along the way. We had it mapped out beautifully, completely ingrained in my soul, an inevitability waiting to happen, and just a matter of having the money to do it. In those days it seemed an incredibly large amount to save, just for the fares alone, and so my mate and I also found second jobs night filling groceries in a city store so that we would be able to fulfill the ambitious amount we budgeted for the trip. Being inspired and energized with excitement, we also felt a little anxious about actualizing our plans, however we were definitely determined that we would be on a flight and heading to our destination, twelve months to the day after our friends had gone.

As the year progressed, it soon became apparent that the other three couples began to procrastinate, losing interest and not wanting to book the flights. Perhaps they had settled back into their rote routines, and maybe they had other priorities in their lives. What had begun, as an enlivened and passionate goal, one that we all sought to achieve, now became a two-man band that only we were resolute to accomplish. In fact, our friends began to suggest that even we may not make the cut and would also change our minds. Suddenly the numbers dropped from eight to two and we were somewhat dazed and baffled by our friends' responses. The combined energy of the group had diluted and we needed to dig deeper for the inspiration to continue with our own plans. We became fatigued from the strained working hours and somewhat daunted and jaded by the major changes we had chosen for ourselves.

Stepping outside the parameters of our everyday life we yearned to embark upon the adventure of a lifetime and to experience the world "out there". I now realize that our friends were merely expressing our own insecurities and self doubts about going through with the project, and they threw us the challenge to check our resolve. We questioned our motives for wanting to travel, particularly as prior to seeing our friends off at the airport we had been organizing to build our home on a newly acquired block of land. We gradually found ourselves wavering and it would have been an easy decision, along with our friends, to also abort the crusade and renege on our earlier commitment. With doubts and uncertainty now creeping into our daily thoughts, creating cracks in our once solid armor, our decision to stick to the plan became tenuous, and we began to weigh up the pros and cons of going or staying. Do we choose to live from our hearts or our logical minds? Do we stay focused and on purpose, or remain in our comfortable, secure, predictable routine; these were some of our most confronting questions.

In the end, nothing was going to stop us from achieving our goal, and we continued to keep faith and maintain our single-minded vision. Our hearts spoke loudest and we held tightly to our initial decision and persevered, not wanting to give up by instead *talking ourselves out of* living the dream. More than anything, we wanted to embark upon the greatest adventure so far in our lives, thereby stepping into our own grandness. Like life itself, the world was our oyster and we chose to experience it fully. We reignited our passion and continued focusing on the initial strategy, after all we had toiled and saved and sacrificed in order to uphold our faith. Nothing was going to stop us.

We left on the same date, a year later than our friends, following the exact route they had traversed. Along the way, our transformation was akin to the caterpillar morphing into a butterfly. We were in awe of the diversity of other cultures and protocols, making new friends from around the globe, working in various positions and exploring some of the most majestic places on planet earth. For us both personally, our lives were challenged, ushering in extreme changes, altering our states of mind. Soul expansion and new awareness was the name of the game, something that we had not expected, much like the earth we were viewing. My life took on an entirely different meaning and I knew, on many levels of my existence, that I was an *integral part* of my new worldview. Two years later I returned home with an entirely altered perspective than when I had left, having learnt more about my abilities, talents, values and my self at large. The choice I had made to step out of the confines of my daily life had led me on a passage of absolute profundity and the beginning of accepting the power I had to create anything in my life, on my own terms.

That inspirational journey reflected my own greatness, as master of my own ship and I returned with new insights, knowledge and familiarity of the world, a much larger world than I had left. Coming back home after having had those marvelous experiences only brought more wonder into my life and I wanted to expand and grow further. I had recognized and broken through my small-minded limitations, becoming aware of how unlimited the world and life really is. By facing the challenges encountered both before and whilst on the trip, I also found within me a fearlessness of living in the world. By stepping out and taking the reins, I learnt that fear of doing is a limiting belief that is easily held onto until we choose to walk beyond it and live with commitment and confidence. When we know how *great* we really are, then we also know that we can be, do and have anything.

Recently I realized the significance of sensing that greatness again. In a dream, I received a profound message; *think like a millionaire*. It was paramount in realigning my thoughts and heart with my passion for expressing my spiritual nature. Next day I immediately referred to a book written many years ago by a motivating author, Napoleon Hill[10], one that I had read many years before. As I studied the material again, I understood the wisdom of receiving the communication within my dream, the power of persevering and not caving in to inadequate beliefs. To think like a millionaire is to be clear and decisive about your main aim in life, to change your mind set if necessary and at all costs, to continue to step towards your desired outcome. I realized as I read the book again that I was well along the path to living my passion and purpose. All I needed was to continue developing my self-confidence and hence my ability to carry out my goal. It was truly another revelation, inspiring me to be persistent and to begin to walk the walk.

Message:

> *Greatness comes from perseverance. It is only when one decides to give in to the illusory fears, frustrations and overwhelming emotions of defeat, that one is lost to the pain of unendurable sorrow. At these times it is most important, in fact it is imperative, to stay positive and focused.*

Do not ever, ever, think that you cannot achieve your dreams and passions. As long as they burn brightly in your heart, the deed is done. How this happens is a matter for the universal energy to implode. All things are given in the natural order of creation and this too applies to your much-cherished dreams. The lessons along the way and the ability to endure and persist are the nuts and bolts of the plan. You must have absolute faith, without a doubt, that the longed for dream you hold, will come into fruition. It is your will to achieve that will make it so.

Do not be put off by the illusory challenges. In total faith and in focusing only on what you desire, your goals will manifest even after the trials and tribulations that beset you. Know without any other recourse that you can all have your longed for plans materialized. They do in fact already exist, on a level that is within your very essence. It is a case of not giving into the apparent obstacles that scatter your path, and instead relying on those positive traits within your very soul that light your way to success.

Do not wither and die along the way, feeling that life has handed you a negative stack, instead rally to the challenges, knowing in your heart of hearts that it is all part of the testing game that you chose to partake in for the benefit of your own spiritual growth and development.

All is well, and there is always a way, to win through any decoy or challenge. You have come this far in your soul's journey and you must surely trust that this in not the first time such obstacles crossed your path. You have experienced life in form many times and have overcome wayward events and issues, and this is the way of the enlightened human. If you do not have the stormy days to contend with, how then can you ever feel enlivened by the perfect, sunny ones?

It is in these great moments that works of art are born. It is in this state of desolation and destitution that humans draw on their very soul's depth and capacity to live fully and creatively through their magnificent and powerful divine energy. When you realize that this is the human lot, then you shall pick yourself up and with courage, strength and commitment, walk the path to victory. Maintaining your vigilance, you shall conquer all fears and discover that you are far more than you ever thought. You are all soldiers of the light and connected to divine truth and love, shining brightly for eternity.

Stand strong in your resolve to master your ship and sail course for the direction your heart yearns to take. Do not be overcome at any point and hold firm in your convictions to succeed. Do not let fear sabotage those most exalted plans. In all of creation, there are possibilities to witness ones self. Whatever your personal circumstances, it is that which you see (observe) around you, that can guide you to better understanding your self.

Loving ones self above all else, you step through your lives in harmony with the divine. You all, each and every being is capable of greatness. You all hold the same loving energy within your bodies and you all resonate with the same life force that created all living things. Be at peace then, in the process, for you can never be defeated, except by your own thoughts that would betray your true and wondrous essence (being). Still the mind and be at one in every precious moment, no matter what is happening. Feel yourself surrounded and infused by the ever constant, loving light of God. Keep your faith strong and stay committed.

Inner Guidance:

Stay focused on your goal, your desires, and never be disillusioned by the challenges that may be thrown across your path. They are just a test of your resolve and if you know that is the case, then nothing will ever stop your progress. Reinforce your desire with daily affirmations, posted around you as a reminder of your determination and to recall how great you really are, already.

CHAPTER SIXTEEN

Knowing your empowered self

Who am I, if not God?

How often throughout my life I have wondered and pondered about being here, in this body, living on planet earth. I always felt that I was connected with or to some thing beyond my mental comprehension, not understanding exactly what, but wanting desperately to know the answer to that *one very particular* question. It was the elusive search for something specific to satisfy me, to help me fit into the world at large, into my world, in my backyard. As a youth, I recall my favourite book was about Greek mythology. Early every evening I would eagerly snuggle up in bed and read one of the wonderful stories portrayed by the many colourful characters. I would be carried off into the world of mythological and magical beings and I felt a passion for the heroines and heroes and the many adventures they played amongst themselves. The 'Gods' who seemed to have such boundless power and hold such significant roles in determining the outcomes in the earthly characters' lives especially fascinated me. I was mesmerized to say the least, and on a deep level I resonated with the philosophies of mortals and gods, all playing their parts in the game on earth.

In those early years of growing up, instead of searching within for the meaning of my life, my time was spent seeking something outside of myself. When only a small child, my parents would attend church and my sister and I would go to the Sunday school, whilst they joined in the mass ritual. Mum would relate the stories of Jesus Christ to me as part of the religious curriculum and I, being fascinated would cling to every word, totally absorbed by the numerous tales of miracles and mysteries that shaped the Christian philosophy. I would never tire of hearing about the journeys embarked upon by those enigmatic crusaders, all in the name of God. As I approached my teenage years however, my life on Sundays, attending worship regularly, became questionable. What occurred to me as I studied through the higher school years, was how there could be so many different religions, with such varying stories, all claiming to know the truth about God, and yet opposing one another so vehemently. How could this be? I decided then that I no longer wanted to take part in an institutionalized religious organization, and that my excitement and passion relating to Christ and God was as easily and readily available to me from home, or anywhere else for that matter. I did not need to be seated in a church pew to embody the spirit and holy ghost of God and Christ the Saviour.

By the time I had given birth to my daughter and she was almost a year old, I knew I wanted to study social science. I enrolled in a university course and set to work to accomplish the first year's subject, philosophy. The workload was much greater than I had expected and having failed dismally at high school, I was determined to complete the year. As I worked through the grueling topics, one in particular, intrigued me greatly. It was 'The existence of God', and a real thought provoker. It stretched the boundaries of conventional thinking, questioning the paradigms within our society, formed over thousands of years, which dictate the terms and agreements we human beings have made regarding God. The assumptions we still make without thought or inquiry, as if what is handed down to us, almost like Chinese whispers, must be true. I loved the subject and it chipped away at my own mindset, bringing to light the differing perspectives of science versus the unsubstantiated aspects of Gods existence. The arguments for and against, the truth or untruth, in the end came to naught. Personally, I learnt that it does not really matter, for in each moment the pendulum can swing one way or the other, and it is only in ones own mind and heart that the answer, the truth is relevant. It will always be an individual choice, depending on the circumstances and conditions applying to each person's viewpoint on life and religion.

Being a very philosophical soul, from then on I curiously meandered in the quest for further knowledge of *my* existence. I was restless and unsettled and after returning home from the awesome and eye-opening adventures overseas, I was seeking to ground myself and connect with a purpose. At an airport while waiting to catch a flight between visits home, I stumbled across, not coincidentally, another significant book that drew me to it. As was typically the case, my hand reached out and there it was, *Love Without Conditions, Reflections of the Christ Mind*11, perfectly positioned on my chessboard of life, awaiting my next move. By the time I had arrived at my destination, my energy was alight with an exuberant passion for living. Simply reading the Author's Preface had done that for me. To quote, "To think of Jesus as being outside of, and independent of your mind is to miss the point. For it is in your mind that Jesus addresses you. He is your most intimate friend speaking to you, sometimes in words, often beyond words." My heart resonated, recalling my connection with unconditional love.

On a deeper level I knew it was time for me to embark upon the inner journey, through thought and deed, responding to a heightened sense of perception shifting within me. I felt the connection with *Christ consciousness*; omnipotent presence, one consciousness and the energy resonated throughout my body emitting tingling sensations, that prompted me to remember who I was as a spiritual being. No longer needing to seek outside myself for the answers, I felt a deep reliance on the invisible, unseen energy flowing through my veins. Faith is the most apt description for the transformation that was unfolding within me. With no visible proof, or scientific analysis, in that moment I trusted implicitly the magical vibrations heightening my spiritual senses, bringing awareness and conscious recognition of being "God". The bible says, *be still and know I am God*. The key word is 'know', not think or analyze or even believe, but *know*. I knew then that it was so, and the simplicity was self-empowering. There is nothing else that compares with the feeling of knowing. The heart opens, the mind lets go and a flood of emotions surface of complete overwhelming love. In the context of the word God, it is used here to describe the *one connection with all that is*. The terminology is irrelevant for it is the energetic essence that holds significance.

As I continued to expand, I could feel the subtle changes and shifts within me, furthered by the supportive messages that enabled my altered reality. I *really* began to live my life full of passion and commitment to my dreams, never realizing the extraordinary journey of awakening I was embarking upon. Never in my wildest dreams did I understand from a human viewpoint, the discoveries I uncovered within me, the unlimited potential, as well as the quiet reservoirs, the essence of which is all encompassing throughout the entire life force. With the deeper connection of spirit, my higher self, I have found peace, love, support and guidance every step of the way. Through the daily process of stilling my often-unruly thoughts and emotions, I have taken the internal steps to knowing and understanding that all is well in my life, at all times. When I opened my heart to join with the magnificent spirit of my being, my God-self, I felt a great sense of family with me, loving, supporting and guiding my direction. At times when I lost sight of the path I had chosen and felt as if I wanted to grab at something else to "fix" a problem, I found myself seeking the infinite stillness and feeling once again comforted and sustained; all fears and concerns dissipating immediately, knowing that *being is oneness with all.*

The light goes on for most people in the darkest moments. Turn the light on now; don't wait for that extreme event or situation in your life to trigger the switch. Live your life now, alert in every moment, fully committed to purpose and fulfillment, and joyfulness. Elevate your energy vibration by attuning to the infinite intelligence that is life and which flows freely within and without you. In so doing, release yourself from the entrapment of exterior concerns and experience the freedom it brings. Focus your thoughts on your desires and feel the power of creation that arises to the surface of your conscious intent. There is no separation between you and life; it is merely an illusion of being in the human state.

Being still and staying present, feeling the simplicity of being, enables me to release the old stories of inadequacy that jump into my thoughts and reside in my bodies, attempting to hold me back and keep me small. In learning to trust my highest direction and hold absolute faith in the process, as uncomfortable as it may seem, I have stepped through doubts, fears and insecurities to expand into my greater potential, consciously holding my energy high and living my life as I choose, rather than being led by conditioned, safe thinking. I give thanks regularly for the blessings in my life and I graciously celebrate every moment.

Message:

Life in all its glory is an expression of divine energy. The source of all creation, it radiates abundantly throughout the universe and lights up the heavens. Humans are an expression of this same energy; ever present, ever conscious. The truth of these words is simple.

When a man unites with himself, it is a glorious reunion (in partnership) with his higher being. Align your selves with this simple truth and allow life to flow in synchronicity and harmony. Live life fulfilled, knowing who you are; loving light beings of divine energy.

You are all connected to this chain of energy and you are everywhere in everything. When you recognize oneself in this state of essence, you then recall those memories of self. As you grow in this awareness you open to so much information on all levels and are inspired by loving presence to recall more of your true identity. In this way, over time, human beings will grow in greater understanding of themselves and the ever-present energy family who resides with them in consciousness.

Living from spirit is the purpose of our lives, and no other. When we return home and begin to live fully from our hearts in spirit, our world expands around us to encompass all of existence. We open ourselves to reconnect to the beauties of nature and the vibration of our soul resonates at a higher, clearer, more defined rate. Filled with love, and from joy and happiness and a gladness to be alive prevail. We are one with all living spirit and feel safe and truly trusting in our life adventure, no matter how troubling it may appear, externally.

The physical world becomes more of what we really want, as we grow and develop, trusting in the one source of supply for all of our needs and mirroring our internal reality. We begin to flow in natural synchronicity with the one energy of life and truly feel blessed for all we experience in the process of living. In gratitude, we coexist with the creative energy that is life.

No proof is necessary when you touch your soul and realize there is no other "you". Spiritual beings, one and all, here for the purpose of expanding your soul, here for the pleasurable journey of removing the disguise, and uncovering your true identity.

Heart to heart find comfort in self-knowledge. You wear the truth within your very essence and you need only to check in with your self to discover all the answers to the questions you seek. The answers do not exist externally of you.

Advancement comes from letting go and opening yourself to the loving light that dwells within. Bound as you are by eons of information derived from age-old sources, you have exalted the information, rather than the "message" hidden in the information. This has resulted in analyzing and intellectualizing the words, rather than feeling the essence in the message the words express.

Having constant faith is your seal and protection in all of your life situations and it always serves you well. Enlightenment is simple; turn inwards and feel the depth of your own loving presence. That is all.

When one feels the truth, the experience is embodied in the essence of the soul and it is on that level the shift and transformation in energy occurs. Live then daily, from the inside out, and you shall surely make a difference in the world. Take one step at a time and move in the direction of least resistance. Stand in your power and connect to the core energy (source) and trust implicitly, yourself, to deliver to you whatever it is you desire. You are the one and only creator of your dreams and the ability to manifest your desires, is completely up to you.

Be fun loving and free and dare to risk it all, to have it all. Break the chains that keep you tethered and free yourself of the limitations of fear and negative thinking. Then enjoy the greatest pleasures that abound in life for your tasting and experience.

The richness of life is therefore the experiencing. It is only the smallness of thought that has shutdown the talent for ultimate creating, and this can be turned around by knowing in your heart that anything is possible and at your fingertips for the having.

Love one another and assist each other to expand into this knowledge, thereby enhancing the lives of all. In creating and manifesting such wonderful possibilities into your life, you feel complete and united with what is.

Inner Guidance:

Unlock the door to wisdom and power through maintaining spiritual focus. Spend time each morning breathing into your heart and uplifting the entire life cycle, making a conscious decision to know yourself on a deeper level of existence. Make the connection a regular experience in your daily life and notice the changes occurring in your physical world.

CHAPTER SEVENTEEN

Being unstoppable

Maintain your stance and have absolute faith

Experiencing the Mystery Tour brought a myriad of challenges into my worldview. So many magical moments offering up curve balls from all directions, and one in particular that was both terrifying and empowering. Whilst in Colorado, we had been escorted to a most amazing and wonderful place on earth called Chimney Rock. It was here, during an incredible climb to the pinnacle, that I confronted one of my greatest fears. Generally, I had thought of myself as being physically fit and agile. The mammoth climb we undertook on that day was for me witnessing one of my deepest *perceived* weaknesses. Even before we set out from the base of the mountain, looking up toward the chimney, my stomach began to churn and I felt the fear welling up within me. The prospect of making it all the way *up there* brought terrible anxiety and self-doubt. I did not feel that I had it in me to do. Most of my trepidation related to *thinking* about walking the ten or so kilometers, up hill in deep snow, something that I, and most of us were unaccustomed to. I dreaded the idea that I would not make it, and also be *the only one* not to make it.

As we were briefed at the base before heading out, I urgently tried to convince myself that I could do it. Self-talk aided to lighten the heavy weight from my deadened legs as we all slowly traversed the narrow uphill path. The first section was gradual and as we began the ascent, I remember breathing deeply and repeating to myself, you can do this, you can do this. If they can, you can. That's all there is to it, mind over matter. Accompanying our group were friends who had done the climb the previous year, bringing up the rear to support the slower, less capable ones. At times as we climbed higher and higher, I found myself stopping, catching my breath again and being overtaken by them. They seemed to be in cruise control and here was I heavily out of breath and dehydrating. I could not get enough fluids into my body, and as cold as it was, I felt hot and very, very bothered. Lee who was with me, keeping pace, and carrying an injured knee, was doing far better than me. He was actually slowing his pace to stay at the rear with me, a constant at my side urging me on. I felt awful, absolutely stressed in every area of my body and mind. The rampaging emotions surfacing from within me were of self-defeat, unworthiness and I battled myself mentally to stay focused and committed to maintain my vigilance. I felt inferior to the others, alone and all I wanted to do was stop and turn around, go back to where we had started and stay there. It was all too hard and I wanted to hide, from everyone else and particularly myself.

I still do not know how I managed it, I felt near tears for most of the journey, mentally and emotionally distraught. I kept asking the back supporters how far it was to go, it seemed like every few minutes. I know I stopped a lot of times to catch my breath and have a sip of precious water, and I cannot describe the relief I felt when we turned a bend and I could see the group ahead standing, laughing in joy at arriving, and looking back to where we had come from. The views were absolutely incredible, three hundred and sixty degrees of magical panorama, and I was moved beyond words at the majesty of it. Our guide moved between us and offered us a reprieve to re-energize with refreshments before moving on again. We had not quite made it to the top yet. What! There was more trekking, further to go? I could feel my heart race wildly again as I went into a minor panic attack; I thought we were at our destination, on the top of the world. Not so. Between my pulsating, throbbing heartbeats that sounded like loud gongs between my eardrums, I could faintly hear him explain to all of us that we had to traverse a narrow saddle, with no safety hand railings, before we would reach the peak of the mountain, the chimney rock. In those few moments, my exaltation plummeted from being relieved and calm, to a tense height of anxiety and *being out of control*. My fear barometer skyrocketed big time, and as we slowly walked in single file, he again cautioned us to take care with our footing as we tentatively made our way across the snow covered, rocky bridge.

I cannot recall a time prior to that particular event that I had felt so fearful, other than an excursion up the Centre Point Tower in Sydney that had me terrified. Perhaps there had been many more, however the feelings of vulnerability and fragility in those moments totally besieged me. I was standing on the edge, so to speak and my body silently shuddered as we progressed slowly toward the summit. One by one, following the leader, we ascended nearer towards the imposing rock formations, approaching cautiously and sure footedly. I kept my gaze focused directly in front of me, never wavering from the course, not wanting to look side to side for fear of throwing myself off balance. Edging closer ripples of relief surged through me, mingled with awe at the sight of those colossal rock monuments before us, their gracious heads reaching majestically for the sky. I knew then I had made it, that I had not given up, had pushed through the mental and physical barriers, to reach that most stunning place in the entire world, right then and there. I was able to breathe freely, to laugh and release the tension, at last, be free from pain. I was on a high, as lofty as those impressive mountains, and euphoric simply being there, and with the accompanying sense of achievement. I sensed the enormous break through I had solemnly undertaken in *doing*, of moving the mountain within myself, highlighting a mental toughness that surprised me.

What amazed me most was learning about the Chaco Pueblo people who had lived on top of that mountain, many hundreds of years prior to our arrival. They had carried all the materials required for establishing their homes up those winding rocky slopes, where we had just traveled, all the way from the base. They had built incredible masonry structures at the chimney pinnacles, perfectly constructed stonewalls and a vast circular, ceremonial meeting arena. It was remarkable and inspiring, an incomparable spiritual experience, mirroring my fortitude. How they accomplished it was beyond our logical understanding. It was a truly mystical journey that we had the greatest privilege of participating in, connecting on a deep level, with the people from a past long gone who had lived atop a mountain in a village, working together in unity, one tribe to create harmony and well being for all.

They had come and gone, disappearing with no apparent reason but leaving a legacy for future generations to ponder and enjoy.

If that hike had not been enough of a challenge, another awaited me several months later. During a sensational course in another beautiful area of the world, I was also presented with an exhilarating climb, of equal proportions. Also participating with another group of people, the ascent was different, this time the focus was to assist each other to reach the summit; along with carrying heavy materials for use once we had all gathered there. As before my fear surfaced at the very thought, and yet it was a far more subdued emotion that arose within me than previously. I had already glimpsed the map, and knew the course of action to take. I now had a familiarity associated with climbing uphill terrains and my perspective had shifted for the new task at hand. On first hearing about the mountain climbing assignment I immediately knew in my heart that I could do it, no matter where I finished within the group. I would make it all the way up without struggle, and I would also *enjoy doing it*, which would be the icing on the cake so to speak.

That is exactly what happened, and after walking for several hours, I found myself in the lead group, feeling pumped and excited. Physically and mentally it was entirely demanding and at times I had to force myself to keep moving, particularly approaching the steepest ascent to the peak. Absolute resolve and commitment buoyed my energy, accelerating my pace, and this time it was I who was encouraging others to keep going. At times I would even retrace my steps to accompany them, urging them to take those few extra steps along the path, to keep progressing. I knew how difficult it could be to assail a mental mountain, for I had first hand appreciation of the quandary. Knowing not to give up, to extend ones' self beyond the pain threshold and continue moving forward, of being unstoppable, and able to give assistance, exactly as I had needed on my first climb. Triumphant feelings pervaded my awareness and it was so obviously apparent that *working as a team* to arrive at the pinnacle was the name of my game that day. Understanding the union between several increases the energy of each one. Sharing in harmony and synchronicity for the benefit of the whole group. I had realized the true meaning of leadership, that of gently guiding, by being there, and serving others, in silent agreement. It gladdened my heart immensely.

Message:

You are unstoppable. Anyone in the world, who has ever accomplished any worthy goal for change and transformation on a deep level, has had to be persistent and strong in their resolve to attain their desired outcome.

Do not let your small, ego mind create doubts and fears in your abilities to finish what you have started. You began by throwing caution to the wind and dreaming big. Stay focused on the bigger picture.

You are being carried on the wings of angels now and you need have no fears or concerns whatsoever. Stay firm in your faith and know that there is much more at work now, than what you can presently "see". This illusion is the problem, so stay strong and committed to your goals. Do not allow negativity to weaken you. All is well, so be at peace.

You have died for less in the past and you are not about to die now. You are always taken care of, in every moment, so stay buoyant and light in your body and know with certainty that this too will pass.

There are so many wonderful reinforcements in your daily life to give you courage and the spirit to sustain you. Maintain your stance and have absolute faith; you are not alone. The enlightened warrior stands firm and can overcome any discomfort because he knows the true value of his power, while surrendering his fears and never ever giving in.

The first impulse when challenged is to go and fix up the problem and to play the small game again, through thinking small and working it all out logically. As you expand your identity to embrace spirit, you feel the support, love and guidance flow through you, bringing solution in ways you could never have imagined with your limited, fearful, thinking mind.

The warrior values the connection with spirit and gives due respect and honour to the guidance and association given by his spiritual family. The way of spirit brings clarity and support.

Embrace every challenge as an opportunity to bring you exactly what you desire. Embrace the challenge to empower you and to give you strength and will to succeed.

I am confident, I am powerful, I am successful and I choose to play a big game.

Go for Gold, you can have it all, because you are it all.

Inner Guidance:

Whenever you are confronted with a challenge, recall your ability to stand firm in the face of adversity. It is only when you choose to give in, that you do not achieve your goal. Have faith in yourself and rely on others around you for support if you need it. Connect with your core energetic power and raise the bar to another level. Push through the fear and know who you really are, supported and guided in spirit.

CHAPTER EIGHTEEN

Begin by practicing

This is the challenge; to be still creating time to sit in quiet is necessary

RELAX YOUR SELF, FOR YOU do not have to do anything. The world spins around in a constant timeless rotation and it always will. Take your time to enjoy each moment and live it fully in present time. There is no need to rush here, there, or anywhere, except when created in the mind with thoughts of *have to*, or *must do*. Constantly doing is man made, and even though in each moment you are doing, *existing in some arena of your life*, even relaxing is doing, and more a *being* experience requiring little thought or mind play. Stimulated by daily routine, we have been taught at an early age, within society parameters, to busy ourselves, or otherwise we may be labeled lazy or idle. I remember the old catch cry when I was just hanging idly around as a youngster, "haven't you got something better to do with yourself?" It was as if one had to be constantly *doing something*. Or even in today's world, people state that they feel bored. I immediately wonder bored with what? I do not, or never have, been bored with living life. Sure, at times I may have wondered what to do with myself, however those days have long gone and I know that when I became a mother for the first time, I would have loved the opportunity to have a few of those quiet precious moments to myself again, of idly hanging around.

Particularly as an adult, I can recall times when life was a constant mass of activity, and then a contrast of slow motion as if nothing were happening. Even though mentally I wanted the pattern to either slow down, or impatiently make it move faster, it seemed as though it was out of my control. The lesson was simple and I gradually learnt to be in step with the seamless rhythm of events and to accept what was. It struck me that in each moment I am partaking perfectly in the scheme of my life experience and to enjoy the condition, no matter what the tempo. The key is to breathe into the moment and decrease the stress levels one can create by thinking of what must be done, either from not having done it yesterday, or worrying that it needs to be done tomorrow. Staying in this state can certainly reduce tension that builds within your mind and body, creating a more empowered feeling. This simple process is like a refresh button within your self, charging your battery and elevating your energy level. Regular practice of stillness creates balance, centering your energy, and is the impetus for greater wellbeing.

I have found that I can achieve far more from a composed state, rather than answering the mental call that speaks of should be up, off and keeping busy. When I relax and release, my breathing slows and deepens and I am consciously aware of oneness with spirit, my higher self connected to infinite life force. My pulse slows and I experience a shift from identifying only with a physical body. In that space it is as if the body does not even exist and a perception of simply being pure, heavenly consciousness is absolutely pervasive. All concerns are void and null, irrelevant in the moment. Heaviness is replaced with lightness and a peaceful manifestation takes up residence within me. Senses, on all levels are stimulated and I experience loving presence emanating throughout my body(s) and a heightened sensation of self.

The more we do from a balanced and relaxed situation, the more we can do. By focusing daily and breathing into your body, releasing the habitual urge to do something, you are able to increase your energy levels and your consequent ability to achieve so much more. Being invigorated, power flows naturally through you, enhancing each cell and bringing clarity to your thoughts. Feeling energetic, you are able to respond to daily issues and pressures from a more heightened environment and to reconnect with the source of creative energy, bringing solution and insight from a broader context. Meditation, exercising, yoga, sport or participating in chosen martial arts brings discipline to your mind, spirit and body, also elevating your energy fields. Eating foods that correspond with your own unique body's requirements is another area to increase your overall health and wellbeing, bringing a happy, joyful approach to how you live daily. Listen to your inner voice to receive guidance about the specific food types of particular benefit to your body.

At first you may encounter some mental resistance to the process, because the old instilled habit must be broken. The incessant chattering mind will attempt to dissuade you in any way it can. Feelings of guilt, fear or anxiety may hinder your concentrated attention and prevent you from maintaining your practice. I refer to this as self-sabotage, and once you bring this into your conscious awareness, you are able to dismiss the unruly thoughts quickly and return to being completely present and relaxed. The old voice of ego will try anything to disrupt your new intention, so be aware and alert to the feelings within you and counter the voice in your head with a positive affirmation, that relaxation is serving your highest good. Learn to develop your ability to "notice" the mind games shaping your thoughts so that you can immediately return to present time, remain calm and continue paying attention. Any feelings such as guilt can come from past conditioning and do not necessarily serve your life now. Ask your higher self to guide you and show you what it is you need to know. And then let go and trust; the answer will be supplied through an inspired idea, dream, sign or symbol pointing the way and bringing with it, recognition within your self.

Living a fulfilled life comes from "being present" and maintaining a high level of energy in your life. In every moment, be fully aware of your surrounds and stay focused on your desires and visions. Be at peace with yourself in all undertakings and choose to do only those things that you love to do, or are drawn towards. Embrace the challenges when they come and step your way through them, moment to moment. A problem is never as humungous as we imagine it to be in thought, and will only reside in our thoughts as long as we allow it. Press the delete button and maintain your position, relax and breathe, releasing the stress as you journey in each moment. Become aware of the hidden areas within you that call out for change and transformation. As you become conscious of old energy patterns arising that may have held you back, intend to release them with loving intention into infinity. The process will enliven you, enabling change of habits, creating new and inspiring ways to direct your life in harmony with who you are, a spiritual being enjoying a human life on earth. Feel the wondrous abundance of loving, radiant power infinitely enfold you. You will certainly live an extended life on earth in this state of being.

Message:

You may feel anxious and have a need to "make things happen" and it is in this state that one must practice to still the mind. It is only a practice of breaking the habit of the mind. Sit quietly for but five minutes, breathing through the anxious urgings to act, and allow for the release.

Regularly practice and eventually you will know and recognize the urge and let it go immediately. It is then that guidance comes from your higher power, illuminating your path in miraculous ways; you will be amazed.

Be at peace with your brothers, all over the world. The history books tell the age-old tales of battles and defeats, of deaths and tragedies and yet this is all man made, yet done in the name of God. How can this be true and so? God's name is only used as a word described by your very selves; your real God spirit and ally consists of the loving light of existence. It is not in God's name that battles are fought, but in man's supremacy to be the best, to beat him self up, in truth.

For he only does this to himself. He alone battles with him self. He really only plays the game alone. And so it is in every situation and crisis that man continues to beat his brains out, trying to solve his (mans') issues and problems. If he but understood that he has bypassed the very essence that dwells within him self that could be of greatest assistance. There are no battles to fight (and win), only the surrender of all things to his own loving source, to shine and heal every situation that exists in his life.

How simple this is. It but takes a slow down in the pace of his affairs and real centered concentration and connection with his inner being, his real self. The lesson is easy and yet frightens the hell out of most men. To take stock and slow down and to even consider the simplicity is such a big deal. When this happens though, the riches that appear are worth the efforts. And efforts they are truly not, but just a simple practice of stilling oneself for long enough, getting uncomfortable and really settling into that most wonderful, peaceful state of rest.

In this blissful state, one will discover the answers to illness, the directions for problem solving, with such ease that it is miraculous. It is the wonder and truth of life and the connection each and every one has with self (the God self) within. It is a practice, done anywhere and at anytime; no need for any shrines, halls or ceremonies; it can be a simple case of pausing one's thoughts and reconnecting in the moment to the ever-abiding stillness within.

Simple, simple, simple, this is the truth. No need for science books, history books, any books in fact. Once the habit of practicing self-awareness occurs, the process is etched in the memories and is easily accessed when the need or desire takes hold in any moment. This is the truth of enlightenment.

Be still and know I am God. Make the reconnection without any other thought attached. No need to strive or try; no need to harp on any other particular practice, only the true one that carries you swiftly to your divine core. In time this process is so natural that one can be in this state of oneness with self at all times, in all situations, thus radiating such peace, love and harmony to all other fellow beings.

Worry not, you are fully supported in love by all and we inspire you to stick to your plan. Even when the external view does not seem to match the internal, it is all in perfect balance for the path you take.

Release your fears and anxieties at regular intervals, simply by sitting in stillness and exhaling the "worry energy" from your being (body). In that moment you have cleared the circuits again to allow the loving energy to flow freely, supporting and nurturing you at all times. In this moment you know that all is well. It is so simple.

The answers that you seek are in the moments. Your need to step further ahead into the future really brings you no relief. It is a futile exercise, as you will see, as you proceed further and further into your inner depth (self). Peace resides there in every moment, always. Have no doubts about this.

With continued use of this applied practice, you will come "home" in any stressful situation, immediately to find your inner peace regained spontaneously. Feel the breath of life flow through your very essence when you are in this state of peace, and release all fears and concerns.

Live your birthright; this is who you are. A work of divine art, displaying your love and light upon the earth, bringing treasures to all others in your sphere and along your path.

Take time to listen and share with another. You have all the time in the world. If you can but uplift another's spirit, then you have done your work.

This is the challenge, to be still. In this peaceful place, one finds the toolbox; the strength, the support, the love, the family and the secrets that unfold a life of extraordinary quality and fun. One must trust, that is all, and totally surrender. Letting go of preconceived ideas and outcomes is crucial to this simple activity. Creating time to sit in quiet is necessary.

Be still, be peaceful, feel relaxed, for the more you attain (stay) in these levels of bliss, the more you open to receiving.

Inner Guidance:

Centre yourself daily, either by meditating, yoga or some form of discipline that suits your energetic being. Focus your attention on observing your thought processes and how they affect your way of life. Connect with your higher being in co-operative alliance with the God within, and feel peaceful, relaxed and energized for the start of your day, knowing that all is well in every moment.

CHAPTER NINETEEN

Children are our teachers

Encourage your youngsters, from the time they are born, to live fully in and encompass the world of spirit

FROM THE MOMENT OUR CHILDREN enter the physical dimension, they are prone to the heaviness of earth bound conditions. They rely on us, their parents to support and guide them through the heavy traffic of life here on this planet. Where do they come from and who are they? Why do they choose us for their parents, and why do we choose them as our children. These are the many questions that one could enquire regarding the identity of our beautiful babies, born at precisely the right time, in the right place, to the right family. We already know them in spirit, and as soon as we sight each other again, the recognition grows from then on and we feel at home with each other, and this was certainly my experience. Generally there is a comfortable association, a loving transcendence, a unique understanding between us. This reconnection is as it is, simply part of our plans, devised by us to meet up for another experience in human form. We all resonate with a hidden depth of understanding and knowledge, of the spiritual formula that unites us genetically as family members, explaining why our links are often so tightly integrated. Our spiritual attachment is our definitive nature and structure, underlying all else. Without knowing, we would feel disconnected and alone, wandering aimlessly through life, as some of us tend to do.

Our children are a blessing of love and light and in their innocence they come forth into the world to remind us of our hereditary, our spiritual identity. They can teach us older, and supposedly wiser souls, who we really are. They help us to remember our own childlike qualities, our relation with simply being in each moment. They rely on us for everything and we learn the art of sacrifice, and to pay attention unselfishly to another's needs. We often forfeit our own desires for the benefit of theirs and learn that giving can be far more enjoyable and rewarding. Being very protective, we would even choose to die, if need be, to save our child's life, or any other persons, for that matter. At an early age, these babes that enter our lives are full of wide-eyed wonder as they purvey their new environment and surrounds. Curiosity is the impetus for reaching out and touching, seeking, smelling the new terrain in which they find themselves. The simplest things can excite them and they laugh and smile without inhibition or self-consciousness. They are innocent and have not yet developed fear or apprehension that would induce them to pull back from expressing themselves wholeheartedly. They are truly a marvel to watch and learn from.

Quite often because of our own conditioned beliefs, it is the learnt role of the parent to dismiss, ignore or be totally unaware of these subtle attributes in their child and very soon, as they develop, he or she also becomes conditioned by the exact same set of rules, surrounds and circumstances. If we could step back and watch and learn, and particularly listen, to what our children say, both in deed and words, our society would change the way it thinks about who our children are, and particularly who we are as human beings. Instead of assessing them from a purely physical, intellectual perspective, we may offer them the choice of growing spiritually, along with materially, creating balance and harmony in their psyche. We would give them credit for understanding and knowing more than meets the eye. Being divine by nature, as we all are, they can perceive life on that level because their minds are yet uncluttered by the information dump they are soon to have. Their line of communication with spirit is pure and their self-expression mirrors that unison. Divinity shines forth abundantly from within them, and that is what attracts us so keenly and devotedly to our children. We will stop in the street to stare at a baby passing in a stroller, or want to have a cuddle, return them a smile, or have a chat, in baby language of course. We are so magnetized and drawn to their loving, innocence because it represents our own loving essence.

If we could but provide more learning centers for our children that resonate with whom they already are by encouraging them to envelop themselves in the subtle deeper aspects of spirit and psychic development, already inherent in them. Our present system is regulated by government bureaucracy and tends to neglect these overall and fundamental elements within each and every one of us. Instead of requiring them to learn general information and techniques that are rarely incorporated into our everyday lifestyles, it would be far more advantageous and valuable to promote the emergence of innate aspects of our spirit, such as our powers of telepathy, our spiritual nature and soul attributes, those unseen senses that operate beyond the confines of our physical bodies. We would ultimately equip our children with insights into the oneness of life, showering upon them the knowledge of the loving, powerful beings they already are and the non-separation that exists between each one. In that regard we would move beyond the need to fight each other over human made territorial divisions. As adults, with a unified perspective of living on earth, our world would become transformed into a society of co-operative populations respecting one another's diversities.

The time is soon coming for parents to recognize and acknowledge themselves in association with their children. Certainly babies and children have specific physical and material needs, to be fed, bathed, bedded, however the innocent soul, the new entity materializing into this earthly existence, comes with a message for all receptive parents. It is a message of love and exuberance for being alive and is meant to rouse the inner child within each of us. It was certainly the case for me as I developed an awakening and awareness of myself through the interplay with my children and it is now extended to my interactions with my beautiful grandchildren. Ultimately, it is a two way street, as we are all interconnected within the whole, the oneness of divine life and therefore here to learn from one another. For most parents, they feel that they are more knowing than their young ones and this can be a misjudgment. At this time in the history of the planet, there are many souls incarnating for the purpose of arousing humanity to their rightful, spiritual identity within the universal system. Bright little buttons, one and all, they are here to serve in the expansion of human consciousness.

Joyful to perceive, it is a blessing that they come to earth at this time, to teach and transform awareness in humankind. Be it unconsciously, we are all influenced on some level by the imprint caused by this latest generation of human influx.

We have misunderstood the purpose in creation, when we ignore the glowing innocence of the baby we bear and who brings us tidings from our homeland. In every case, a child represents who we ourselves are, the spirit of divinity, the precious, joyful, loving being who is wise and knowledgeable. It is the gift from God (source) that we chose to receive for our own purposeful awakening. We all have the ability to connect with our spiritual world through our association with our children, so embrace them fully as the jewels they are and hence you will be embracing yourself. We are spiritual beings, and once we open our hearts to encompass spirit, we then choose to live a life fully from spirit, in every aspect, and then we come to experience wonderful transformations in our physical reality. Look upon your life as a wondrous expression and extension of your spiritual self, and then you will fully enjoy the marvels that life offers in every precious moment.

Message:

> *Your world is a magical mix of seen and unseen factors. What you perceive in the physical is only a small glimpse of the reality. It is the unseen energy that is predominant and therefore of the most sublime.*

> *The world you do not see is rich in everything and supports your journey whilst you are in the physical world. You can touch, taste and smell the energy of the "other" world if you choose and this is why many innocent young ones are able to do just that. They do not carry the impositions and restrictions in their thoughts of not being able to. They can easily connect with the unseen energies and they laugh and delight and feel the safety in doing this.*

> *You older beings have simply shut that part of yourselves down to accommodate the conditioned society in which you live and were led to believe by your elders. Very soon this will reverse itself and come back to a time when you do indeed encourage your youngsters, from the time they are born, to live fully in and encompass the world of spirit.*

The dark clouds are beginning to lift on this side of life and it is nearing the time in the evolution of humans on earth that each will retain those early memories and be encouraged to live a life full of spirit.

An amazing new world is opening and available to all now, if they (one) can accept this into their life now. You are all able to reconnect to your spirit and to the abundance that is in everything and flows through your self.

Claiming your own identity with (in) spirit is the first step.

Inner Guidance:

Our children fly the colours of our soul and if we become attentive to what they have to say, and the ways in which they behave, we can profit from their wisdom, which in turn reflects our own.

CHAPTER TWENTY

We are all intuitive facilitators

A breakthrough in spiritual awareness on earth is manifesting a host of powerful attributes and abilities within each human expression

I RECENTLY EXPERIENCED GRIEF AND sadness when my nephew tragically died in a road accident. It was a heart breaking incident for the family, as he was only 30, still in the prime of his life, and he departed this earthly existence prior to his parents. Losing a child, before we ourselves pass on, can be something most of us feel is the most terrifying event to ever happen. And it could well be, if we think of it only in a physical sense, as a total ending to someone's precious life, and of never seeing them again. From my perspective however, it is another opportunity to break through the mental shackles that hold us prisoner of our own fears. It is a chance to understand our deeper relationship with the sacredness of life, and consequently our correlation with all beings in all dimensions. Even when our loved ones *disappear physically* and move to another place in space, it is still possible, if we make ourselves available, to feel them with us and to communicate with them directly. If we are open and receptive, we are also able to perceive them in bodily form, glimpsing their spiritual blueprint, their translucent soul body.

Such was the case with my nephew's departure from the earth plane. The day after his accident, whilst at work, I heard him speak to me. A specific song entered my thoughts "Jesus loves you", repeating over and over, along with thoughts of him floating through my mind. Even though I had only met him once, at my mother's funeral, I knew him on a spiritual level and I recognized his voice when he said, "Aunty, I have fallen off my bike and I don't know where I am". I felt his innocent youthfulness, present in spirit, and I responded by saying, in thought, "You are alright, call for Granny to come". As soon as he did, he told me that she was moving towards him, and in that precise moment I sensed he was comforted. Jolted from my thoughtful ponderings by his voice, the sorrow I had been feeling left me immediately, and I knew in my heart that he was happy. He felt light and alive, and accepting of his circumstances and I felt pleased that he had made the transition peacefully. The next morning as I slowly awakened in bed, sitting up I glanced across at a beautiful picture I have on the wall, one given to me by my mother, and I caught a glimpse of both she and my nephew standing radiant together. All was well, where time and space are concurrent, and the past, present and future are now.

I felt more deeply for my sister's sadness, for her loss and the acute pain she felt at his departure. I thought that if she could make the spiritual advancement, she would also feel differently, knowing that he was safe and close to her, one with her and only an unseen dimension away. She would still experience the heart wrenching feelings of losing a beloved one, not have him walk through the door and greet him again, and she would understand that he lived in the same sphere as her, only not available through our finite physical sensory system. To open ones' self to perceive that which is invisible, yet vitally alive, is like taking the lid off our well-developed linear thinking and allowing our mind the exploration of traversing the higher realms of existence. When my mother died some years ago, the set of circumstances I experienced were the catalyst for developing more deeply my own intuitive sensory system. Lee and I had only recently married and were overseas on our honeymoon. Staying in London, with only a couple of days left before heading home, I received a phone call from a friend to say that mum was critically ill in hospital. Realizing her deep concern that mum may not recover, I was frantic to get home as soon as possible.

Frustratingly, after several failed attempts to change our flights and depart immediately, we had to wait it out for another two days. I felt on edge, restricted and totally helpless being on the other side of the world with absolutely no chance of winging our way home. I had to bide my time and I remember quietly saying to myself, repeatedly, mum just hold on until I get home. Mid way through the flight, in Singapore, in the very early hours of the morning, I rang the hospital and asked how mum was. The nurse told me that she was not doing well, in a lot of pain and then surprised me by asking if I would like to talk to her. I expected her to be inaccessible and to merely get an update on her condition. When we spoke, she sounded drained as though the pain was too much for her to bear, reflecting my own painful inability to be with her. I asked her to hold on a little longer as we were almost home. I was able to tell her how much I loved her and she said she loved me too, and then the call was over. My heart felt relieved that I had snatched the moment and that we had lovingly shared, if only briefly, with each other, ushering in a peacefulness that I had not felt since being told of her illness. Several hours later, we arrived on Australian soil at 6.45am, and commenced the arduous two hours drive home. It was shortly after leaving the airport that I got an intuitive message to call home. In my heart I already knew what I was about to hear, for I had felt mum's *pat on the shoulder* and understood that she had made her departure. It was as if she had prolonged her own journey until we had landed safely back on home soil. It was a devastating blow to my heart, coming so close to being with her physically, but missing the boat so to speak, and not having the chance to see her ever again, in the flesh that is.

That night, again in the early hours of the morning, I awoke with the feeling that there were three of us in the bed. I could strongly feel mum's presence as if she had just walked into the room. Lee also wakened, without my prodding and said he had just been escorting mum around Paris, where we had spent several days of our honeymoon. He said it was exactly the same as if we were walking the streets again, only this time with mum close by our side. She had always wanted to go to that historical city and see the many significant architectural structures and view the exquisite art pieces on show in the Louvre, and now she was flying with us, accompanying us, one with us. I realized then the profundity of time being simultaneous. There was no time, in reality and mum was with us no matter where we were. She had wanted to say her farewells in another time zone and in an exhilarating fashion. She had not died at all; she was merely in another space that we, in our physical state, could not see. She was pure consciousness, communicating with us that she was alive and well and having a ball. I felt inundated with emotion and tears flowed, along with a gladness knowing that she was having fun and experiencing worldly adventures; now free to travel wherever she pleased. Neither earth time nor a painful physical body restrained her spirit as she soared freely. It was a very special moment for me, bringing a wonderful sense of renewal and lightness to my heavy heart. That magical occasion had been utterly amazing, and it was only the beginning of even more bizarre events to follow, leading up to the funeral. More reminders to us that she was not gone; her essence was alive and well, and part of our own.

Over the next few days, she guided us to choose the style of farewell party she wanted, particularly the music for the *celebration of her life*, and it was another synchronistic run of events that unfolded. Her simple coffin was totally covered in and overflowing with the most spectacular array of bright, exuberant flowers and we brought them back home and adorned the kitchen bench with them. We filled a glass with her favourite white wine and left it near the flora for her to sip on during the course of the festivity, and at days end it was only half full. We were guided to listen to the most marvelous music that we had not heard before, and we knew we had to play it at the celebration. On first hearing it, I had broken down sobbing again and I knew it was significant in some way; it was so poignant. We borrowed the CD and played the same particular song over and over all day long. At the end of the wake, I tiredly wandered outside, taking the cover of the CD with me, wanting to know the meaning of the words. Having not heard of Andrea Bocelli prior to listening to his music, I found his voice was utterly divine, sending shivers through me with its intensity of emotion. We had repeatedly only played the first song, Con Te Partiro, which he sang in Italian. As I sat and began reading the words, I gaped in astonishment, and my heart swelled with love and appreciation. The meaning of the words was, *Time To Say Goodbye* and I was deeply touched by the sentiments sent from mum through that beautiful song. We went and bought the CD and I played it constantly for quite some time. We realized that the last song on the disc was also the same as the first, only sung in English, with Sarah Brightman accompanying Andrea in a duet. It was truly a meeting of all our hearts.

Knowing we are spiritual beings having an earthly experience, makes the world of difference in the way we view life, our own and others. We all have the ability to open ourselves to our psychic potential, to read the varying frequencies of life. We just have to intend it. During my lifetime here, I have seen many psychics, wanting to be told what lies ahead in my future. Most of the time, I already knew what was being channeled to me anyway and I was merely seeking validation. I thought the reader was the only one able to access the data, as if they had a secret formula for tuning in. And yet they were really only mirroring my own potential to inform myself. As one unit, being joined by thought bands; we are all capable of aligning our frequency to infinite intelligence. I liken it to plugging into the power point and lighting up a room. We are alight with life's energy and able to contact abundant and absolute intelligence in any moment in any time and space continuum.

These shared stories of *passing over* are more intensely felt because of the extreme gamut of personal emotions, combined with the surreal state one particularly feels when someone close dies. In terms of access to our infinite power, each of us can claim that anytime, in any moment, as we have done for eternity. This is not new for any of us, merely forgotten. Sharing lovingly, one with each other, we become open vessels for giving and receiving constantly. If we acknowledge who we are, through thoughtful introspection, we deposit our self into the all knowingness of life and recall our part within the entirety of existence. If we fear, or doubt, we may block the process and then question the realities in our world; not a bad place to be either for it will throw up agendas for our mind's reflection.

In today's world, with the advent of Harry Potter for example, and many other wonderful fantasy stories alive and well, the message is that we have the mental capacity and know how, to step closer towards, the so called realms of impossibility, by believing we can. What we see as fantasy reflects our imagination, inner vision and much more that goes beyond our mental knowhow. We are drawn to the story because it excites us and we relate easily to it. It is just a matter of growing beyond ones limited thinking mind and stepping into the genius you already are. Like the Harry Potter stories, you merely require a classroom where you can learn to express your innate, spiritual talents regularly and ground them in your everyday life. Once you know you are able to freely, without inhibition or judgment, express who you are, you will consciously expand and spiritually grow at a rapid pace. We are all only limited by the way we think and if we understand that we are not limited by anything, other than our often trivial beliefs, and our own critical judgments, then we are well on the way to breaking through the old patterns we hold, and opening the door to our spiritual inheritance, of understanding who we are.

Message:

> It's an amazing time in the life of all humans on earth. There is so much activity and electrifying energy around the globe. This is because of the shift in the evolutionary process taking place and the enabling of a higher vibration sequence on the planet.
>
> At this auspicious time on earth, humans are feeling the effects of these changes on a deep level. There is an undercurrent of personal transformation and this is felt at a cellular level. The brain is a physical component of the body; the mind is a portal to the subconscious state of being and therefore the connection with spirit. In stillness, the mind acts as a transport to another area of awareness, not perceived when the mind is thinking through the brain wave frequency of external activity.
>
> Life is dramatically changing for many and this is apparent through the many challenges embracing society at large. In a spiritual sense this is applauded, as awareness and consciousness in each soul expands to encompass this changing vibration.
>
> The elements of energy in nature are responding to this shift in experiential occurrence through adverse weather and climatic changes, as well as planetary, structural shift.
>
> This is all in alignment with the plan of creation, and is a new frontier for the planet and all of its inhabitants. In a world of learning (lesson), this is essential for the formation of greater planetary awareness and the human experience. Nothing in life is ever stationary and the constant, changing evolutionary process of life is a natural phenomenon.
>
> A breakthrough in spiritual awareness on earth is manifesting a host of powerful attributes and abilities within each human expression. Spiritual awareness within each human brings greater scope to the expansion of the planetary system.
>
> The awakening of each soul to understanding their origins, that they are connected in spirit to the source of creation is the clarion call now. An imprint at a cellular level has left its mark on the current incoming soul group, which signals the beginning of a new era of humans, being in harmony and balance on earth for future generations to come.

It heralds a time of personal responsibility, spiritual awareness and unity amongst all beings, in a new age of peace and abundance.

You all have an innate ability to perceive more than you think, and it is only your conditioning to social parameters that prevent you from understanding and learning the techniques. However, the changes that are happening on the planet now, on a deeper level of people's subconscious, will enable a growing awareness of life in other forms to manifest. By other forms, we mean that you will be able to "see" other life in dimensions previously undetected by the human eyes and senses.

On certain levels, humans are already feeling that there is more to life than meets the eye in the physical form, and here we do not just mean about the after life dimension.

The present chaotic and disruptive energy patterns are a reflection of the underlying shifts shaping this new era. In reality, all is going as planned and much can be celebrated for these shifts and disorganizations now taking place in your world (individual world).

With loving hearts, embrace these changes, for you are an elemental part in the whole process. The planetary spirit resonates to the tune of your loving presence and sings its own song in accord with the changing energy vibration present now and growing (expanding).

Give thanks each day for the nourishment that the earth provides us, and respect and honour the life that is the planet itself, for it is an energy system just like your self and is vibrating in alignment with each and every entity walking its surface.

Inner Guidance:

Understand that you are capable of reading energy, as an energetic being connected with the entirety of all that exists. It is a natural ability that we all own and simply requires an intention to open one's mind and heart to the omnipresent vibration of love.

CHAPTER TWENTY-ONE

Abundance in all its forms

Life is the fuel of worth and abundance in every scenario

When my children were aged eleven and eight, we shared Christmas day with their Dad and his family. An Aunty from Sydney, who hardly ever saw the children, was also visiting. She brought with her two humongous boxes laden with toys for each of them, and I mean gigantic, storage size boxes that were chock-a-block and overflowing with wrapped presents. She had obviously felt a need to make up for other times of absenteeism. Initially, the kids were over the moon with excitement and could hardly wait to dive in and start ripping those parcels apart. About half way through, the room was an absolute jumble of toys, books, clothes and games, ones they hadn't even stopped to look at, and quickly the unwrapping frenzy began to loose its appeal. I sat on the floor with them, assisting to remove the wrap and wade through the gifts, attempting to view the contents. It was as if they were more intent on just ripping the paper off, and the toys became secondary. Even though the intention of giving had been exemplary, it had also been excessive and was way too much for their tiny minds to entertain, and for their senses to really enjoy. Their exuberance waned very quickly and the pace of opening the gifts slowed to a halt, the unwrapping instead becoming more of a chore. While they disappeared to play outside together, many of the gifts remained unopened and were gathered up to take home later.

They had their day in the sun, so to speak, and receiving the stupendous volume of material gifts offered all of us a broader perspective, particularly about what was really valuable in our lives. Both knew they had been given far more than their wildest dreams could have conjured up, and that alone was abundant. In fact the toys they were gifted could easily have supplied an entire classroom of children, and we spoke about sharing the stash of goodies with others less fortunate. In its way, the experience provided the opportunity to consider the importance we placed on *having things*. Previously, their urgent demands for wanting would have been painfully persistent. Now it seemed less of a priority, an overdose of materialism, similar to feeling sick after eating too many sweets, or an overload of junk food. Also we discovered that being given so much tended to dilute the inherent value of a thing, creating a blasé acceptance, rather than heartfelt appreciation. The lessons we shared on that particular Christmas morning were indeed very valuable. A few *loved* items can be everything; less can be as meaningful, particularly if it is desired and embraced with gratitude.

In contrast to that abundant episode, another eye opening encounter awaited me whilst traveling in India with Community Aid Abroad. Participating in a community leadership program it was indeed a very privileged occasion to view the other side of the coin. Commuting through the countryside towards a local village, along a narrow rutted roadway in an old decrepit bus, I was amazed as I gazed from the window to see a group of young children playing underneath a huge billboard. The earth beneath it was littered high with rubbish and debris and the outlying homes were frugal. The whole area was brown and deplete of any greenery. It was a scene of desolation. What impressed me however, was the nature of the children present. They were laughing and swinging on ropes and appeared to have not a worry in the world. They looked "poor" by our material standards, but in my heart I sensed an aliveness emanating from their small beings and jovial conviviality. They expressed pleasure purely with what they had before them, amply sufficient to satisfy their young minds and hearts. They were full of spiritual activity, enjoying the simplicity on offer. They had nothing else in their world to compare it with, and in that state of being they enjoyed enormous freedom and happiness.

As we continued to traverse the landscape, experiencing Indian culture, I witnessed a firm, unwavering unity within family and community life, which touched my heart immensely. These were people working together from the grassroots, with little materially except for what they grew and handcrafted. The unification within their community created agreement and balance amongst each other, and they coexisted harmoniously as they cooperated for the good of all. It was then that I viewed my own circumstances differently. I understood the meaning of abundance from a very different standpoint to the one I had grown up with, in western society. Instead of needing to work independently all of your life in a "have to" job, and striving to own your home, both for the purpose of creating security, I realized that abundance is personal, a feeling that emanates from within, encompassing many positions and possibilities and not necessarily only something of tangible value. Abundance can be sharing time with family and friends, or listening to music that resonates with your soul, or tantalizing your palate with foods and wines of your desired choice. Whatever brings happiness to your world and those around you with whom you share it, seems to me to be the essence of living abundantly, and without doubt, it flows outwardly from within your spiritual core, and not the other way around. Feeling grateful for who you are and what you have is abundance. Knowing your abundant self is abundance. It just is.

Therefore, abundance does not necessarily mean ownership of any thing; after all, we do come with (no thing) into the world, and also leave with (no thing). Therefore, why do we strive to own so many possessions? It seems to me that when we have them, we then want to have something else, some thing better, or alleged as better. Like the saying, "the grass is always greener on the other side", we never seem to be satisfied with what we have, and consequently who we are. Is this not another belief, or learnt pattern fed us by our ego? Presently our society appears to be engrossed with materialism; especially as advertising of goods and services constantly bombard us with items we supposedly cannot do without. We are lured into believing that we will miss out on some thing or other, if we do not own things, and have what our fellow human may have. The pressure to maintain a lifestyle full of goods and chattels, which are highly dispensable, is huge. We appear to value our selves against what we own and if we are not owners of things, then we ourselves feel that we are less valuable in our society. Some of us are called "poor", based on what money and possessions we have, and yet we are all equally blessed simply being here, alive in this world with all the opportunity available to generate, with our own free will, whatever we desire.

Now this is not to say that money is not of value. In terms of supplying us with the means to exist materially throughout our lives, it is of essential value. It is also energetic, as we ourselves are, enabling us to live within this physical dimension whilst supporting our needs. It is a part of our vibrating self, reflecting our inner spiritual wealth. It is another *tool* for our learning if we view it in this light, and we can manifest an abundance of it. Once again, it depends upon our own mindset and beliefs about having, or not having it. Understanding that we are already abundant beings is a major aspect in the co-creation process. Part of my life lesson has been about recognizing this attribute within myself. In that enlightened arena, understanding that we are products of our thoughts in relation to attracting or repelling money is highly beneficial to an altered awareness. I have had the benefit of participating in my own amazing journey with money. Without the challenges to bear around my own financial prosperity, I would never have embarked upon opening my consciousness to patterns of behaviour that have stretched my ability to hold onto money. I have learnt that focusing my attention on getting money can push it further away, whereas having faith in my higher self to guide my every step opens the abundant flow of entirely everything I need in every moment, without the need to dwell on the how and why, or the fix it aspect.

Another stream of abundance within our world applies to academic achievement and emotional fulfillment. Some of us have the ability to learn easily, providing a platform to proceed to positions of power and prestige within the working arena. Again, within our society, we value this highly and remunerate those positions with superior monetary profit, along with extra bonuses and benefits. We send our children off to school at a very early age to begin to learn these very same external procedures of procurement, based on a material framework and reference. The pressure is placed on them to also achieve and accumulate what we have; mimicking the very same agendas we ourselves hold. We are rewarded if we do well, and if we do not, then we are either made to feel like dummies, or reprimanded. The rewards are meted out in some form of material item, and if we fail the system, the punishment can bring enormous emotional consequences for our futures. How many young souls have been stripped at an early age of their abundant self-confidence, because they did not enjoy, or fit into "school society". It only takes one humiliating experience to shut down our potential ability and deter us from moving forward with poise and grace. Our spirit can be shattered at a very early age, by events that do not support or acknowledge our unique talents and extraordinary individuality.

It is our differences that often challenge the system by which we live, within a society of such high expectation. Our school system does not yet fully reflect our spiritual identity, except for religious studies, which can be restrictive and selective by its very nature. Other than a few topics like language, science and mathematics, rudimentary for navigating through the passage of daily living, most of what is taught at school is about understanding facts and figures, purely general knowledge of events either past or quite irrelevant in the scheme of our adult life. When are we going to introduce disciplines into our educational institutions about who we are, the grander who we are, and not only focus our children's attention on what they must become when they grow up. If we can guide the young mind to understand the potential it has to create anything, simply by connecting spiritually and thinking (from the heart) with passion and aliveness, then the worldview could eventually shift to encompass one of great abundance, in material, emotional and spiritual wealth. There are many wonderful subjects available, still labeled alternate, which recognize our spiritual capacity and capability. Why are these topics still not part of the general school curriculum, starting from the very first teaching a child experiences.

We are all abundant beings, all uniquely different, and all absolutely talented. As we understand who we are on a deeper level, we acknowledge abundance in other ways. It is no wonder that we love to travel to places that permeate us with feelings of beauty and inner wealth. Nature plays the magical part of mirroring for each of us, our own spectacular nature. As human beings, we are imbued with the essence of life energy, which we are free to use to create wealth in abundance, materially as well as on all other levels. Go out and explore the world, for it is absolutely abundant and connects us with our wonderful self. Choose to live passionately, and focus your attention on what you desire to have in your life, be it a loving fulfilling relationship, a happy functional family, or all the money and wealth you can imagine creating. Simply connect with your particular passion, picture yourself attaining it and then take the action steps toward manifesting it into your reality. Know that you are divinely united with the source of your bountiful supply and you have nothing to fear. You are the key to your own enjoyment and happiness.

Message:

The fast pace of life and the accumulation of things is not the only way. Without doubt, one can create and attract anything into their life for whatever purpose, and if these things feel good and bring joy and happiness, then all is well. On the other hand though, if in the accumulation, the things are not rejoiced, or enjoyed, then what does the purpose of this serve?

When it is realized that life is abundant on many levels, then there will be less required of the material and more of the spiritual. Then the seeking will shift from the external to the internal, and peace will reside and joy and happiness will abound within each one.

The tangible is not real but man-made and it only exists for the pleasure of the ego. It has no substance but to satisfy the yearning for greater pleasures that are hidden deep within the soul.

Let it be known that you are all wondrous beings of the light and you do not need to appease yourselves with the pleasures of the flesh (physical reality). Once you come to realize this truth, then you will really come to enjoy the simple pleasures life has to offer. You chase the hum drum stuff, as if it is the only reality on the planet and yet by so doing you miss the entire point of existence, which is that of love, harmony and oneness. What is it that you really strive for?

Do you really know when you spend your time looking outside instead of in? When will you realize that there is never a need to discover the truth of who you are in the ethers of self-discovery? You are all blessed and guided by the true one, which is your self, your higher source of creation.

Treasures are unlimited, growth is unlimited. When one knows oneself truly and trusts that life is the fuel of worth and abundance in every scenario, then one can continue on the path with full realization that support and love are always at hand from spiritual dependence.

When you know this in your very soul and being, then everything is always alright. There is never a moment needed to be spent in fear or concern. The flow of your life will harmonize with spirit and provide you with all your needs and desires. This will happen in easy flow, with no apparent effort or struggle. You will have put your faith totally in the presence of love, which is your essence and that which exists in every moment.

Grace and gratitude flow through you, and then you really are alive and in synchronicity with the God within, bringing great beauty and bounty.

Inner Guidance:

Wealth of any sort is a personal experience; so focus your mind on creating that, which makes you feel elated. Extend love and cheerfulness to all others around you, being of kind heart and compassionate in your outpourings. Happiness is the guideline to feeling successful and fulfilled; so fill yourself with pleasurable experiences that bring joy to your heart, thereby reflecting your inner world.

CHAPTER TWENTY-TWO

Whales are calling

Are you listening?

THE WHALES ARE CALLING US to remember who we are. These giant, docile and peaceful members of our planet are on a mission. They want us to see and hear them and recall our spiritual worth, our greatness in the universal picture of life. Such magnificent beings of love, we attune to their significance and recognize our own innate being through them. They sing to us from their hearts and if we listen, we can hear their messages of hope and inspiration. They are saviors, come to remind us of who we all are, providing us clues to coexisting harmoniously in this special environment called earth. If you think about it, generally we humans absolutely abhor the idea of these wonderful creatures being decimated and we go out of our way to help protect them from annihilation. When they are beached in massive numbers, we spend days and nights applying ourselves frantically to help rescue them, enabling them to continue on their journey. We are magically drawn towards their prominence, without thinking why. Yet it is not only the whales, but also many, many hundreds of natures' beautiful animals and creations, that inspire us to aid their plight.

So why do we feel this way? I feel it is because they mirror our own cause within the cosmos, and the sensitivity we feel to being extinguished from our own existence. When we witness the whales being slaughtered unnecessarily, we connect with painful memories of previous atrocities, along with current events occurring around us simultaneously. We want to save them, thereby saving ourselves. These spectacular mammals come with a special purpose, to help raise our energy levels and to facilitate our receptivity of being powerful. They are part of the majestic plan of life, bringing great weight to the purpose of life that we all share. Attuning to their predicament, we discover our own salvation. In loving whales, dolphins and all of life's myriad creatures, we essentially attune with love of self, awakening compassion for one and all that exists. Within nature is the wealth of our being personified to infinity. How could we harm, or destroy that which resides within us.

I like many others, have had the great honour of experiencing whales firsthand, both physically and also whilst in dream state. Once when Lee and I were casually strolling along a panoramic ocean pathway at Lennox Head, we sighted whales approaching the bay from the north. One could not miss the giant cloud like spurts exploding high up into the airways and our attention was immediately drawn in their direction. Seating ourselves on a nearby bench, we watched, totally absorbed, as slowly a mother and two of her young calves swam close up to frolic in the shallow waters, within easy range for us to clearly discern their antics. Mesmerized by the playful activities and remarkable sounds of the giants, feelings of exhilaration enlivened us and we felt in tune with them. They lingered for ages and then mum turned and slowly steered into deeper waters, approaching the headland where surfers were riding on boards, also enjoying the waves and no doubt the whales too. As she distanced herself from the calves, we watched spellbound as she retreated, calling them to get a move on and follow her lead. Then they were gone from sight within minutes, as they dived deeply into the dark depths of the ocean.

The intimate union, the family connection between them had absorbed our attention, for it could have been any family splashing in the ocean, or a mother and her children playing at a park, for the behavioral interaction was so similar. The kids were having a *whale of a time*, and when it came time to leave, mum stopped the play and called the two to catch up with her, a familiar pattern we can all relate to. Silence remained between us long after their departure, as we warmly savored the remarkable experience we had shared. When we did venture to express our feelings, it was with immense gratitude at having witnessed such an engaging natural event. More than anything, I was mindful that the world we live in is a stage upon which we are constantly reminded of our wondrous existence, showcasing who we really are. Every connection with life and nature is mirroring our soul, our essence. We are always, always shown that we *are life* and we exist primarily for the purpose of recognizing our self in all that is. My heart blissfully sings when I recall that, *being here*, in each special moment, is simply for that purpose.

Sharing another involvement with whales, a truly different one, was whilst I was in dream state, in the subconscious realm, and the reality of the experience was as valid as if I were awake now. After the dream, reentering a conscious state, I was still involved within it and knew that it was a message of substantial significance. I was in the ocean, below the surface and a considerable distance from the beach. I am the whale, and on surfacing I was looking back towards the shoreline, seeing the rolling hills of the land spread before me. I am conscious of being a whale, exactly the same as having consciousness of being human. I know that I am alive and with purpose and participating in the manifestation of earthly life. The profundity of the dream showed me, even reiterated to me, the reality that we are all threaded energetically, completely whole, within existence. If we choose to listen and pay attention, we are each capable of consciously tapping into any state of being. We are the whale, and any other entity if we but realize it, through association. Divinely manifested in the image of the creator, being one with all, perhaps our primary purpose exists in this simple recognition.

Often I see in the media that the whales are moving closer to the beach. There have been many incidents reported, but the one that I watched and which brought great delight for me, was when a fisherman in his small tinny was calmly floating not far off shore when he was under shadowed by a single whale's visit. Encompassed by the dark mass of the whale's body, the report showed an aerial shot of the boat floating over the gigantic silhouette, the enormous shape of the whale outflanking the boat many times and making it look minute in comparison. Then the whale surfaced, within close proximity to the side of the boat, taking the man by total surprise, and bringing him face to face with the giant sea animal. How incredibly amazing, and no doubt overwhelming, to be looking eye-to-eye with such a gentle, but huge mammal? It was an incredible story, bringing of course a great deal of attention with it, highlighting the special affects that whale encounters have in our lives at present. When I notice these events happening now so regularly, I cannot help but think they are very purposeful. The fact that we are so impressed by these rendezvous with whales is enough for me to consider their purpose on earth. Most of us feel an undeniable love and respect for them, along with an affinity for their calm yet powerful natures. In some way it represents our own might and gentleness that we recognize, and therefore protecting their place and space is as vital to us, as it is for them.

Message:

> Many people are now experiencing a shift in consciousness and so the time is very fortuitous for this material to be written and shared. There is an undercurrent of misaligned thinking about what is happening on the planet and it is time for a reassessment of these things.

> Why do people only see what is in front of their eyes, and not open to the wider peripheral view of the unfolding processes really occurring around them. There are no coincidences or accidents on the earth plane and every thing; every event has purpose in it, even if you choose to deny its validity.

> Every situation has a hidden lining (agenda), much more than can be seen by the human who is looking only through the vision of fear and anxiety. That is why the message must go out; that love resides in each one's heart and through this connection with self, life can be healed, as each human heals himself.

> The journey must begin by checking in with the heart, and not only the mind, particularly the voice that loves to trigger off fear at every opportunity. The process will gather momentum and the outer world will change, as the inner worlds of humans change.

> Know this one and all, because life on the planet is in a turn around position, and all that it is going to take, is for each person to grasp the context of his own power to create for himself a world of love and peace which resonates with his being, and that which he truly desires in his life.

> Be in alignment with your spiritual self and not out of alignment with your thinking mind. Watch the things you think and the words you speak and make them only that which offers support to your higher values, thus offering the same to all others with whom you interact. This will send out the message that life is cherished and precious and worthy of the utmost care and consideration, everyday, every moment of your living life on earth.

Feel the peace and goodwill radiate from your enlightened being, feeding the same energy to all others, to your brothers and sisters on earth and all living creatures. You are all worthy and deserving of the abundance that is life and that which is who you are.

You are all loved, you are all wondrous beings and your outer lives can reflect this. The choice is yours to make. Become aware of who you are and how you play the games in your lives. In everything, is love abundant.

Inner Guidance:

I attract everything into my life for my own unfolding and discovery of self, and this occurs in natural rhythm with being present in each moment.

CHAPTER TWENTY-THREE

Peace on earth

Simply Awakening

IF WE REALLY DESIRE PEACE on earth, we must firstly awaken to the peaceful essence residing within our own heart. There is no point in continually living a life of dysfunction and conflict with our family, friends and neighbours and at the same time advocating for a peaceful world. These do not go hand in hand. The outward gesture toward peace on earth simply implies a need to establish serenity within your own personal reality. The work must firstly begin in your own backyard, within your own inner being for results to appear in your outer world. Being at peace with yourself, your life will reflect and radiate your own tranquil consciousness. In every moment, be aware of how you interact with all others around you and within your sphere of influence. Do you offer love, honor, respect and consideration to all you meet, or are you angry and frustrated and acting out your inner conflicts, transferring your own energy onto others.

We pretend that everything that occurs outside us is separate from us and that we have no control over certain events. We often buy the stories we see and hear through the media and then feel angry, annoyed and frustrated that we cannot fix things to our satisfaction. We want to blame the politicians and anyone else for what appears to be happening all around us. For example, Attention Deficit Hyperactivity Disorder in children, along with teenage rebellion, are escalating issues within our society now; why are so many kids having such a difficult time, at school, at home. We look and think that it's a problem with the children, but maybe they are mirrors into our self, particularly our dysfunctional self. And the Gulf war, why are we participants struggling in a game we do not want to play. We all have free will and if we are demonstratively affected by external events, it indicates a time to take note of the area within our own emotive self that suffers. The healing begins within and moves outwards. Being prepared to address our personal reactions responsibly, our perception shifts and as a consequence so does our worldly view.

Several years ago I had the enormous privilege to explore India with Community Aid Abroad. For ages I had been a supporter of their humanitarian causes throughout many third world countries. I received a flyer with my monthly newsletter, recruiting passionate people to embark upon a Community Leadership Program. I had yearned to travel to one of the many countries that I constantly read about, to investigate first hand what life was like in those often obscure and unnoticed places on the planet. I wanted to understand how people lived and worked in a community environment. I desperately wanted to make a difference in the world and so I applied for the program, and was overjoyed when I was accepted to participate on such an amazing journey. Prior to flying to India, the selected group met in Melbourne for a 3-day orientation, where primarily we were trained to understand the cultural differences between our own western world values and the long held Indian traditions. Fascinated by the many enriching variances between us, from the simplest greeting to the way we eat our food; it was of paramount importance that we fully comprehended the subtle and appropriate behaviour whilst in the company of any Indian person. As representatives of CAA, it was an integral aspect of the program and vital that we displayed a high level of respect and honour to those customs and its peoples.

During that time I learnt much about India, much about Community Aid Abroad, its programs and people, and most importantly, much more about myself. One of the processes entailed numbering in priority of perceived importance, a listing of twenty or so world values. Of highest significance to me was *Peace on Earth*. I reasoned that if everyone living on the planet had the same mindset, we would each individually create the necessary conditions for its establishment. It would mean an end to hostility, to war, to antagonism, to dysfunction and it would involve being personally responsible. I placed it at the top of my list then, as I still do today. As was the case, it was also the number one priority on the CAA list, and I considered the inference very seriously. The only draw back that I could foresee, as a priority, is if individually we could not all agree, given our extreme differences in religious and cultural belief. I envision manifesting peace in the world, through intending to hold inner peace and radiating that outwardly to all others. Collectively as a human race it would require full participation, and in my heart I feel it is achievable. For a spirit of oneness to exist within this energetic and diverse world we share, it is absolutely essential for unification amongst us all. Since then I have sought to be harmonious within myself, not always an easy task. I understood then, that peace on earth, the external view of my own quintessential being, was entirely up to me to create. Through intention, with heart and compassion, I know it is possible.

Consciously step into your own awareness and take responsibility for creating your world. See how the dynamics of your being, bring a degree of either happiness or turmoil into your daily life. *Make the choice to ask your higher self for guidance*, and listen for the answers. *Intend to create peace* in your life in every possible way. Remember that anything is possible, as the creator of your own experiences. When we play a small game, we get very small results. Believe in your ability to change your life, for it is not up to anyone else except yourself. Learning that you are a spiritual being in human form helps to put perspective on the way you look at your circumstances, and also empowers you to step into the often neglected, non-physical reality of who you are. By thinking peacefully, expanding your reality, by intending to live harmoniously, it is possible. Pay attention to your reactions and responses to all that occurs around you. Recognize your self in action with your thoughts. Step back and connect with your spirit, listen and learn. Be non judgmental of others, for they show you more about you than themselves.

As you strip away the many false layers hiding yourself from your true identity, you also come into enlightenment. You begin to feel differently about yourself and your world. You choose to clear the debris from your sphere that no longer serves you and are in touch with your own powerful being. It is really just another opportunity to evolve and to understand that the fundamental nature of life is self-nurturing and loving, as are you. Everything is a state of mind, and if you desire peace on earth, then make clear intention to think, act, and especially to *be at peace with yourself*. As you focus your attention, so you create your reality. Partaking in the India experience was monumental for me in understanding that aspect of myself. We can all do the same if we decide to. Open your mind to believe and have faith in humanity and the process involved in choosing benevolence over turmoil. At this time in our human history, the people of the world are still looking outside for outcomes. It is now time to look to one's self, touch the spiritual force that emanates from within, to change your outer world. This process simply starts from the inside out for each and every one of us. Life in your reality, is a reflection of who you are, and more particularly, who you think you are in each moment. And so it is.

Message:

> *Today is a fortuitous day for all mankind. It is a time in the history of earth life when so many wonderful changes are taking place on so many levels. Humanity is waking up to a new dawning of spiritual energy beginning to become apparent in many lives. It is a time of great change, even though humans may not yet be aware of this.*
>
> *Life is an abundant pearl, waiting for the time when humans decide to open the shell and take a closer look inside; awakening to the magnitude and magnificence that greets them in their seeing.*
>
> *The spectacular dawning of human evolution on the planet is just a matter of time. An amazing transformation is unfolding in people's lives and more and more are drawn towards an establishment of higher ideals and values that unite one with another, and another, in peace and harmony.*
>
> *Growth and expansion is inevitable, as agreements made on a subconscious level are now beginning to pierce through to conscious awareness. The time is now, for a recollection and recall of why we are living on this beautiful earth, at this particular time in its history.*
>
> *There are no actions or events of coincidence and the people in your lives are all there as a matter of contact with you, often to open your eyes to who you really are. They reflect the "you", through their loving words and actions and even with the "not so nice" occurrences, which really do serve you in a way that triggers a questioning within you for a greater answer to "Who am I?"*

Your life is a sacred journey in self-discovery and when you realize that each one incarnated on earth at this time, has the same life energy and the same lessons, then you know and understand on a deep level, that you are all the same.

You come to aid one another and this in itself is such a gracious act of giving. Even if you think not, it is so. When you begin to feel the depth of who you are, your soul self, you touch the core of not only your own self but all else as well. You are a human consciousness in constant flow, like the ocean tides that come and go, as a sea of love.

Suffice to say, that this phase in human evolution is another step up the wrung of the evolutionary ladder on the planet and it is a joyous time now, as you all stand at the portal of change in consciousness. You feel the vibrational shift within your own essence and so you know at the core that it heralds a new, wondrous beginning of expanded awareness within humanity, ushering into your physical realities amazing possibilities beyond your present comprehension.

The weight of the world is lifting. Lightness appears and is apparent to many souls. It is a time of awakening to the true identity for each one, and the group. It brings forth a greater awareness of the possibilities for peace on earth and amongst all of the living inhabitants upon its surface.

It is the beginning of a new world, one that will usher in new concepts for living richer and far more fulfilling lives. The bonds that connect you all will tighten and there will come many who assist in many new ways with the changes.

The changes will be most evident in the simplest ways. Firstly, coming from each individual will be the awareness that we are all one and connected in spirit. Not only that but that we do not stand apart from God. God does not reside outside of us in some physical form, as widely believed within the religious doctrines.

Rather, once individuals realize this simple truth, that he/she is part of God (within oneself), then this will bring enormous shift in consciousness and then long held doctrines will crumble and be replaced with radiant beings, shining their inner most lights upon the world.

Replaced with love, fear will drop aside and allow for great wisdom to surface within human consciousness, leading the way to enlightenment and change. Breaking free from the shackles, people from all walks of life will come together in harmony and like-minded energy to create a wonderful existence upon the planet. Starting from within each one, this will explode out into the heavens bringing forth an abundance of loving energy.

It is simple and it is the way. Let go of struggles and trust in who you already are; loving, light beings of the infinite creative source. Let all men know this news and be gladdened of heart, for it is the truth and cannot be shelved anymore in the deep recesses of the soul.

It awaits an awakening in each and everyone, a marvelous expedition into one's essential being, a glamorous new beginning and a turning of the tide.

You heard the call to passion and have found peace in the process of living your divine destiny. What pleasure this brings to all of heaven.

These words flow through you, for you and all who come to read them and are inspired by your longing for peace on earth and goodness for all mankind. With your loving heart you have opened the door for these loving messages that bring forth a magnitude of gratitude and appreciation from spirit.

Be gentle, caring and cooperative with all those you meet on your path, for each is reflecting yourself and they also benefit from your growth and development. This is the key to living in the human persona; giving and then more giving.

Peace on earth is now inevitable, as the growing consciousness of all humanity takes up the mantle of self-hood and turns on their inner light. In loving peace we all reside, the rest is just a matter of the mind. Love one another and all else is taken care of, for you are all loving beings of the light.

When one and all, are all giving, then there shall be peace on earth.

Celebrate, and love the unfolding moments that bring you untold treasures for your pleasure. Focus on the good, be grateful for all that you have and let all else slip away.

Touching the blissful stillness of life within, one can feel the magical mystery of life; the aliveness and tranquility of existence.

Imagine a million, billion souls emitting love and peace in a world of apparent chaos. What a change this would bring to the earth and all of its inhabitants.

Be in peace.

Inner Guidance:
> *We are all brothers and sisters of the light, living for the purpose of spiritual growth. Here and now, feel the depth of peaceful energy that flows through your veins, and give thanks for the eternal wisdom you hold of knowing and understanding this.*

CHAPTER TWENTY-FOUR

Love is what truly matters

This is the message for freedom, divine light and love is who you are

I AM SO GRATEFUL FOR everything I have in my life; sometimes I am truly amazed by the beauty that surrounds me and which vibrates within me. I am truly blessed for so much, a wonderful partner and friend to share life with, one offering me the necessary components to enable me to see myself as I hold beliefs and patterns around sharing intimately and trusting myself implicitly. An array of friendships, some old and treasured and others new and inspiring, are a wonderful blessing. My children who are now young adults embarking upon their own special and unique journeys. They give me much to consider about my own experiences growing up with them and how it impacts on their lives today. The unconditional loving support they always offer is a beautiful reflection and reminder of the deep connection we share. Then there are my beautiful grandchildren who delight me with their spontaneous actions and loving natures. They are the souls who now come into life on earth with more capacity to live fully from spirit. When all is taken away, it is the love that flows between us that is the most precious gift of all. This is the basis of all relationships, of life itself and can never leave us. It is what unites us all eternally.

I am so grateful for being and knowing my union with spirit and the divine energy that flows abundantly through me and which is me, and for the loving guidance I feel and receive from the *unseen*, alive and present beings who abide in spirit, lighting my way and supporting my journey so gracefully. For this I am eternally grateful. I know this in my heart for I speak with them and know they are a constant presence with (in) me. Walking hand in hand through the maze that is life, it is a pleasure to know the support and love I feel is true. They are the oldest friends I share my existence with and have been with my conscious expression throughout time immemorial. They guide my way when I feel at odds with my purpose and I have met them on occasions when undergoing major transformations. In the darkest moments, I perceive them with me and know that I am not alone. They offer love and encouragement, and in this life experience they are generally referred to as angels. The messages come clearly and often bring warmth and comfort emanating from the heart, or tingling sensations through the body. Certainly, they are as real as you and I and simply exist in a dimension of heightened awareness. They are one with all, as am I, and at times of difficulty, they prod me to remember to live from my heart, and to express love unconditional.

We all know what love feels like, it brings us delight and happiness, it lightens us up, carrying us into the heights of ecstasy; it is invisible in its characteristics, and yet we do not hesitate to recognize the feeling that love imbues us with. It is simple and profound and the most natural attribute that resonates within us. The energy of love can sky rocket us to the stars and beyond, for when we are in love and our heart is full and overflowing with the beauty and majesty of those feelings, we are capable of anything. We feel compassion and want to give unconditionally from a whole heart, one that does not doubt or fear. We do not stop to think, for we allow our emotions to carry us on the wings of confidence and trust the processes shaping our relationships. We surrender to love and want only to reciprocate those same feelings, as we meld with another human being, and they meld with our self. In that moment of complete and unbridled sensation, life has great meaning and opportunity, and we feel on top of the world. We transform into the butterfly, as we soar in self-belief and capability. There is nothing in the world that compares to *being in love* and yet this is our natural form, our essence and when we are in love, we are reminded once again of that fact. There are no words to describe love, it is the basis of all our associations, one with each other, and sweeps us forward in life in the most brilliant ways. It carries us home and warms the way, shining a light of pure bliss within our being. It is transcendental in nature and when we love another, it mirrors our love of self.

While in the human form that shapes ones existence on mother earth, we are all free to experience whatever it is that draws us towards it. This means that everything and everyone that we attract into our life, forms the basis for our ongoing journey of unfolding occurrences. Coupled with this, is a formulation of predestined programming, so to speak, that places each of us in exactly the right place and time for our brief undertakings, whilst on earth. Within the programming that we all uniquely usher into our life model, is the capacity to choose events that can assist in spiritual growth and development. It is this way for all and on the deepest level we have the ability to discern exactly what we came to do, or be, recognizing our capacity to uncover our exceptional and glorious self amongst the vaster nature of all that is. Being part of this brilliant design enables us to think in ways that create an *abundance of loving experiences and relationships*, along with the challenges. When we *see* our self in this light, we recall that we have lived before, igniting the spark and spiritually amplifying ourselves to higher dimensions. There is no doubt in my heart, that we are far greater than we can possibly imagine with our finite physical mind, and so we *can* bond with our higher self to enable this process. As always, it is simply a matter of sustaining our light and feeling the loving presence of creation radiate throughout one's being.

There are no accidents or coincidences in anyone's life and the point is to encourage you to understand the lesson that is impregnated within the situations and circumstances of your lives. When events occur which seem catastrophic, there is a good reason for this and if you can attune with your higher self to uncover the meaning, then you move through and beyond the human state and recognize the lesson for what it really is; an aspect of your spiritual growth. On a deeper level you are being assisted through every process by a loving higher energy, call this *higher self*, as well as other light beings that are ever-present in your company, even if you cannot discern their presence, or feel them with you. This is so, and a great tribute when you acknowledge their divine loving presence which flows through you, as part of you. Realization came for me one day as I was driving up a narrow, winding dirt road and as I turned a bend, rapidly heading towards me in the centre of the road was a large 4WD vehicle. I had no time to think and yet instinctively I veered off centre to the left, knowing I was heading on a collision course into the vegetation lining the edge of the road. I had no other option and certainly I had no physical capability of preventing the car from smashing into a thicket of huge trees. Incredibly and abruptly the car came to a dead halt, only a fraction away from impacting, and in that instant I received an image of *someone* placing a hand in front of the car to avoid the extreme crash. Time and space shifted, were non-physical, irrelevant to the scene, and a wave of triumphant energy washed over me. It was so acutely obvious that a force beyond my physical means had intervened. I breathed a great sigh of relief and felt a peacefulness embrace me.

In these situations, one discovers a subtle truth within life that opens a magnitude of love, revelation, faith and companionship, felt always within your heart and being. Unearthing a meld with spirit that is omnipresent, enriching and supportive, as you travel an earthly path through your maze of pursuits. To acknowledge spirit at this level is a most rewarding and consoling human experience. Amazing grace, stillness, and gratification encompass you always and you walk hand in hand with love, every moment of your day. From then on, as you feel you are *at home*, when situations occur in your life that may be upsetting or distressing, you *know* that everything is really all right and in proper order, in each and every moment, in the unfolding plan of your expression. Instead of feeling shattered from an incident, it is easier to acknowledge and accept the situation, knowing that there is a grand purpose beyond your thinking ability, within it. The most incredible synchronistic experiences occur, and when something that you thought you wanted to come about does not, you can let it go and surrender to the moment, knowing that the plan is much bigger than you can ever conceive of, with your mental, rational thinking. This is when miracles shape your life and you really start to engage in the most remarkable conditions and life changing events. There is nothing more to do, having increased awareness, expanded perception, and wholly accepting spiritual support.

This is not blind faith, yet it requires an element of faithfulness in the hidden intelligent life force that radiates throughout your glorious being, and all else. It is more about trusting your spiritual self to guide your way. Opening your heart to welcome oneness of love between you and your fellow man, even the stranger who passes you along the street, or in the shopping centre. Realizing that you are not really strangers at all, that a common thread, one of abiding energy, attaches you one to another. It is no wonder that when situations happen to endanger us or someone else, we immediately forget our smallness as human beings, and launch into our higher self. We find great strength of purpose and connection that *seems* to appear from nowhere, igniting a spark of divinity and proficiency that knows no bounds and is capable of great feats of strength and endurance. This is love in action, stimulating us to understand who and what we are attuned with. It is spiritual intelligence extending its arm of authority to guide us every step of the way. It is only when we return to our daily life that we tend to forget the significance of staying linked with the core of reality and living from that place, without separation, from then on, always.

Message:

On the ladder of life, you discover the enormous scope you all have to create your world of abundant colour and glory. You are able to shine and glimmer within the safety of the all encompassing loving energy of life; without restraint and chains or heavy burdens of any kind. Without toil, of the human kind, where only light and love abound in natural harmony with all that is. This is the message for freedom.

Be openhearted in your giving. Know the value of service and kindness to each other. The foundation of love is in these attributes of human nature. The light of love flows through the human vessel and adds value to all those who feel the warmth and goodness from another. It is so, even if they are not open and aware of receiving the loving message given in deed.

Be an anchor for love to flow through you to others and in so doing the healing begins. Too busy and caught up in the busyness of life, as a matter of perceived "have to", most humans do not respond to, or receive the loving energy sent from the angels on earth whose job it is to give love.

Maintain your purpose and continue to give love and kindness to all you meet. Be ever mindful of your purpose that is to touch people's souls with unconditional love and support. This in thought, words and deeds, is received even if it is not physically apparent. This is the power of intention and the divine energy is delivered nonetheless.

Be a vessel of loving inspiration always. Shine your heart-felt love around the back blocks and into the darkest corners, illuminating the beings in discord with themselves.

Healing energy through intention is also sent and received in the same way. It is a simple matter of transferring thought waves of intention to the person(s) who you visualize.

Knowing this without any doubt, it is received by the higher bodies of the recipients. In this way, we are able to send blessings anywhere, at any time to individuals or groups and assist in the healing process.

The message is still the same, and always will be. Love is the way, for self-first and then in union with each one of your brothers on earth. The ripple effect of this beautiful energy is expanding daily, momentarily, and is magnificent.

No more suffering, just a united, harmonic convergence of all souls in loving peace and beauty. We can all do this work, simply done, in the presence of quietude and intention; that is all.

There is nothing new; love is the way, and always has been and always will be. Your love supports your journey; that is all. Have the courage to live the life you deserve. Risk it all in pursuit of the dream of love, which is itself you. When you love, then love you are, and all else comes together.

To translate from spirit, to human mind is always a matter of interpretation and therefore the energy that we convey and the message that flows through to you is one of pure love, felt in your heart. For in truth, if all humans, being, can open their hearts to feel the message we send, they would simply feel love. Love for self, for life, for truth and for each other and the planet. The beauty and bliss that is conveyed through love and opening the heart to receive, is <u>all</u> that we ever want humanity to feel and know.

You are all beings of love, entities of light energy and your purpose on planet earth is simple. It is to unite in one, each with the other and to expand this loving energy into the ethers of reality. Each time this happens, the universal energy receives the loving energy and rejoices in pure delight, you have no idea.

United in harmonic balance, uplifting the energy vibrations of all beings within the universal system, this is the plan of expanded consciousness. There are no limits to existence; therefore there are no limits to the human, being.

An element of love is compassion and to be compassionate in your pursuits is to be aligned with all others in co-creation, in a caring, respectful manner.

The deal in life is to live fully; harnessed to your own powerful, loving energy and stepping into the reality you create through positive intentions.

The energy of love exists to ignite the spark of life, each and every one manifest in physical form, returning in perfect form to whence it came in due course. This is the science of life, the quantum patterns and blueprints.

Blessed with every resource within our being, we can create anything, out of everything, for we exist in everything. Our capacity to create is infinite and in being in total trust and natural flow with the source of all being, we can easily manifest that which we desire.

Abundance is our being, and our birthright, not just reserved for a few "lucky" individuals, but for each and every one of us. We are all one with the loving source of abundance and all deserve the riches available in life.

Happiness is yours in every moment, if you choose it. Peace resides within your heart as you feel contentment with your self. A move into a new paradigm of self-exploration is yours and all of humanity.

New world, new abilities, new accomplishments, new, new, new, as you jump off the cliff of possibilities and potentials, you are free to choose, to live fully risking all, or to live from the fear zone of what if?

Go for gold and test the boundary, love guides the way and illuminates your path always; divine light and love is who you are.

Inner Guidance:

Love has no limitations; it simply is as it is, an innate expression of self. By loving ones self, one then has the capacity to extend love to all others in meaningful and joyful union.

CHAPTER TWENTY-FIVE

Perception

The simple truth is to be found from perceiving life inwardly, rather than outwardly

IN SUMMARY, THESE STORIES ARE about me; about my life experiences to date, and in essence are no different from any other persons stories. Specifically, I share how through them, I awakened to my greater being, my higher self. I have especially highlighted the challenges of breaking entrenched patterns of behaviour holding me in check, especially fear of being able to accomplish my dream of inspiring others, a burning desire I have always carried within me. I believe that we are all capable of achieving that *one burning desire, or life mission* that is within us to manifest in this lifetime, as long as we continue to pursue it, no matter the length of time it may take and the number of *seeming* obstacles that may overtake it. It is within us all, to have riches beyond our wildest imagination, if we do not give up on the dream, as long as we do not become distracted from the path, and do not allow our unruly mindsets to sabotage our plans. *This is my perception,* and certainly all of the above were emotional or mental issues that I had to firstly recognize and burst through, step by baby step, at one time or another. I discovered that once I had made up my mind to grow spiritually, *emphatically decided* to push through the fears and doubts that sometimes clouded my view, sapping my confidence, it was very easy to continue on the path I had chosen for myself.

The truth is very simple. It is to *be who you are*, expressing your divine spark in the form and fashion that fits uniquely for you. We do not have to play any other game, other than being truthful in heart. Follow your heart, for it will not lead you astray. Combine it with a mind full of aliveness and positivity and you will not look back. The quality of your life depends upon it; so do not hesitate to claim your power by connecting with infinite intelligence, the creative force. When you join with spirit to ignite your passion into material manifestation, the way will be made clear as you step into aligning with your deepest desires. Be at peace in this knowledge and stay present in the now as you continue on your journey. The path is always brightly lit for you and there is no need for mental anguish and struggle on your part. Let go and let the guidance of your God self be the road you take, and remain resolute at all times. Be still and patient, with the knowledge that all is well, in each moment. One of the key messages I received when I first began channeling was instrumental in reinforcing once again that we are great beings of unlimited love and light. I was experiencing self-doubt at the time when the following beautiful and inspirational, reassuring words brought with them change and transformation into my life.

Your life unfolds magnificently, even when you think otherwise. There is so much that you do not see or comprehend, however when you give intention to know yourself and grow spiritually, that is exactly what unfolds in your whole life. On all levels you are changing and growing and this is not always apparent when you are looking through eyes only focused on physical form. Seeing is believing is a saying that is not confined to the physical realm alone. Seeing through the eyes of your inner bodies, your third eye, is witnessing other dimensions from the perspective of your spirit, or higher self. It is felt from a deeper understanding and awareness and the manifestation in the physical realm is seen as a change in your circumstances, lifestyle and emotional state. It is in the surge of life energy and felt through your sense of contentment, comfort and joy. In a physical sense you know that life is different because of emotional shifts in your body. Since you have begun your writing, the changes you have undergone are miraculous. You have let down your guard, your barriers connecting you to your higher self and we, in spirit, congratulate you for the courage to do that. You have trusted in the divine guidance you gave yourself, through the knowingness in your soul and through your heartfelt feelings that you could write. It only needed you to begin.

In the entire world, there are many who lack the courage, for whatever reason, to begin. And yet, as you have found, it is the greatest work you could embark upon and it gives you the greatest pleasure to feel the fulfillment of an inner yearning. The lesson is to trust yourself and your own guidance and to take the action necessary to commence and hence embark upon the journey that is deeply etched in each human heart, and which often cries out to be heard, and begun. Even in the knowing, the task is not necessarily easy for humans who hold onto the old conditioned concepts of the mind. It is a constant process of bringing awareness of the truth to the forefront of the thinking mind and maintaining a level of continuity and persistence in the course of being vigilant to the task.

By affirming your intention clearly and passionately, you will proceed and commence the journey you wish to instigate. Taking the first step is always going to be the one of most resistance and then gradually the flow of the process builds momentum and you have begun what you have put off until now. There is no better time to begin anything in your life than now. From small beginnings, come great works of art. Life in all its wonderment is so precious. Life is only ever abundant and offers the riches to those who are prepared to step out in faith and discover and explore its mysteries. Beauty prevails in every moment, in every corner, in every atom of being and it awaits each and every living being to step into the eternal, blissful state of existence, through spiritual identification and awareness.

Be prepared to shed the cloaks you no longer need to wear. They shroud you in darkness and as they fall away, you become more and more aware of the loving light of life shining upon you, through you, and from you. The more you peel away the old, unnecessary layers, the richer your life becomes, on all levels. Your inner light radiates a glowing, warm love to all and you feel enfolded within the all-encompassing love of divine energy. Your world opens like a blooming flower and you perceive everything through new eyes of gratitude and appreciation, and there is not a thing in your life that happens that does not touch your soul in a gentle, loving presence and purpose of being. Your heart expands, filling you with amazing vibrations of peace and harmony that permeate all things. You feel humble at awakening to the total beauty that life is, in every moment. Open up your hearts, for peace abides there.

We are all one and the same, melded from the same substance and breath of life. The only thing we need to do is acknowledge ourselves as being this truth. This is the simplicity of our place here on earth and we can elevate our energy to balance our spirit with our individual humanness. How often do we perceive other people being better than us, or famous and out of our league, or having more materially than we do? We watch them and read about them, and yearn to be like them. Whilst we place them on a pedestal, we feel separate from them, and mostly we feel that we could never do, or be like them. We compare our efforts with theirs and then shrink away from completing or continuing our goal for fear we will not be successful. This has certainly been my own view of the world at times, the illusion that seems more real. However, in reality, a part of us actually melds with them and we live our life through them instead of realizing that we can also personally achieve our own greatness by following our inner voice and guidance. It is this perception, from an external viewpoint that would keep us small, shattering our dreams very quickly and immobilizing us with fear. By perceiving our self from a spiritual aspect, we know that we are the oneness, incredible, infinite, all pervasive, and it is enough. We create one step at a time, no matter what that entails. It is after all our own game we play.

Message:

> *The simple truth is to be found from perceiving life inwardly, rather than outwardly. Take a quiet moment, every moment to reconnect to your beautiful soul and realize the truth of who you really are. The key to everything good in your life, is living lovingly from your heart.*
>
> *As you open your heart to receive, the advancements towards you in your life are miraculous, in every aspect. In the recesses of your heart are stored every opportunity, every potential and possible outcome of your dreams and desires. Your life unfolds and expands to supply whatever it is you love.*
>
> *The time is ripe for humanity to let go of the veil that has hidden the wonders of the existence of self in all its glory. It is now up to each one to turn inward and take a deep look at who is hiding behind the veil (illusion) of self.*
>
> *The unwanted fears, and illusions of security will fall away once this journey of inner self is begun and the result will be an amazing transformation in the outer world, one which shines with new potentials and possibilities to follow ones heart in creation of what one wants, instead of taking the "safe path" lived from years of conditioning.*

It is the intention to live more "fully alive" and to have a quality of life, which is the impetus to create the change. The line is crossed and the unfolding of awareness of who you are commences and with it the power within surfaces to serve you on your awakened journey.

Let not fear stop you, instead break through the illusion by staying in the feeling and knowing in your heart, the way is guided by a loving higher self, supporting every step you take. All you need is within you now; the love, the joy, the happiness and once you feel this, then peace and harmony reside as constant companions with your being, in every moment.

There is no wishing, only being. Correlate the past and the future now, for it all exists now and in this you know, and it guides your way. You know it all and this is attested by your intuitive thinking. By attracting to you what you desire, you simply step into what already is, in each now. There is no need for a sense of urgency or anxiety in wanting to have the future exist now. There is only now.

Happiness awaits you now; joy awaits you now, in every moment it exists. Contentment then resides within and flows from you toward your fellow man. This impact is monumental in the evolving process, for once the loving energy spreads from one to another, the process and the results are astronomical and felt on all levels of existence.

The key to living a fulfilled life is being happy in each and every moment, continually knocking on the doors you wish to open. Knowing within yourself that you are capable of creating anything, even the universe! This is so because you are the all in everything, the supreme being of creation.

Your love and appreciation of life draws to you an abundance of wealth on all levels, you only need to feel the love flowing through you to know this is so.

Life has purpose and we feel uplifted to live a full and energized experience, able to create from our power (source), the life we really desire. Free from the boundaries of the physical dimension, we can travel to the extremities of existence and live abundantly from faith and knowingness.

You are able to lead your own way now, in full realization that you are the creator, the maker of your own realities. Now that you come into full realization and discovery of your own divine purpose and potential, you are able to maintain your level of attunement to this energy expansion within your being.

Walk through your fear and find abundance and support. It is the way, and the only way to mastery of your mind. The old patterns that you find reflected to you in your life are only challenges for you to recognize faith and trust within your self.

Why not jump into the deep end of life and prepare to meet with the most rewarding, explorative adventures of your life. Do not get caught up in the everyday, so called securities of job, lifestyle and customary comings and goings, rather than stepping to the edge of existence and jumping off the wall of outstanding, exceptional life experiences?

Step out of your head and into your heart, once again, for this is the only place to find peace residing. Peace is a feeling, stemming from absolute faith in whatever is happening around you. To be at peace is to be in love.

Begin by loving your self, in every situation. Let go and receive.

Inner Guidance:

The picture is bigger than you see, the plan is bigger than you think, so just be, and enjoy the journey of your own unique discovery in the world that you create; so simple.

ENDNOTES

1. Manna—From Wikipedia
2. Visit the Kryon website at www.kryon.com
3. My Place in Space by Robin and Sally Hirst
4. Why Men don't listen and Women can't read road maps by Allan and Barbara Pease
5. The Four Agreements, A Practical Guide to Personal Freedom by Don Miguel Ruiz
6. The Secret by Rhonda Byrne
7. The Passion Test, The Effortless Path to Discovering Your Destiny by Janet and Chris Attwood
8. Mystery Tour conducted by Brendan Nichols Events
9. Spirit of Nature, The harmony of the Five Elements: a path to healing by David M. Bell
10. Think and Grow Rich by Napoleon Hill
11. Love Without Conditions, Reflections of the Christ Mind by Paul Ferrini

www.ingramcontent.com/pod-product-compliance
Ingram Content Group UK Ltd.
Pitfield, Milton Keynes, MK11 3LW, UK
UKHW040626270325
5179UKWH00013B/167